ALAN TOMS

Lessons from Jeremiah, Genesis and Exodus

Contents

I   Gems from Jeremiah

1	JEREMIAH'S CALL	3
2	MY WORDS IN YOUR MOUTH	6
3	FIRST LOVE	10
4	LIVING WATER	13
5	THE KNOWLEDGE OF GOD	16
6	THE POTTER'S HOUSE	19
7	THE NEW COVENANT	23
8	THE FIELD IN ANANOTH	26
9	THE RECHABITES	30
10	GOD'S SUFFERING SERVANT	34
11	BURNING THE ROLL	38
12	ZEDEKIAH	42

II   12 PICTURES OF CHRIST IN GENESIS

13	12 PICTURES OF CHRIST IN GENESIS	47

III   THE TABERNACLE IN ONE HOUR

14	INTRODUCTION	67
15	THE PATTERN	71
16	THE COURT AND THE GATE	75

17   THE BRAZEN ALTAR OF BURNT OFFERING   79

18   THE LAVER   83

19   THE CURTAINS AND THE COVERINGS   86

20   THE BOARDS   90

21   THE GOLDEN ALTAR OF INCENSE   94

22   THE GOLDEN TABLE OF SHEWBREAD   98

23   THE GOLDEN LAMPSTAND   102

24   THE ARK AND THE MERCY SEAT   105

ABOUT THE PUBLISHER   110

MORE TITLES FROM ALAN TOMS   111

I

Gems from Jeremiah

1

JEREMIAH'S CALL

Jeremiah served God at a very dark time in the history of Judah; it could hardly have been darker. The ten tribes of Israel had already been taken captive, but that desolate land to the north of them did not seem to have a voice for Judah. They still pursued their evil ways despite all God's warnings. The little nation God loved so dearly was running headlong into destruction and disaster. All kinds of evil were rife among the people. Idolatrous rites were practised on every high hill and under every green tree (Jeremiah 2:20), God said. The country was full of temples erected for the worship of Baal. The poor were plundered, murder and adultery were the order of the day.

Amazingly it was in Jerusalem where God had His Temple that the evil was at its worst. In fact, His Temple became the headquarters of Baal worship. Its courts were desecrated by the images of heathen gods. "The Temple of the LORD, the Temple of the LORD", they cried, and yet within sight of that Temple the most abominable evils were taking place (Jeremiah 7:4,30).

The days were hard when Jeremiah was called to serve. God told him even when He appointed him to His service that the people would not listen to his message. Their hearts were stubbornly set to go their own way and God knew it, but before His judgement fell He must warn them again of the consequences of their sin. So once again God spoke to them, and whenever He speaks He looks for a man to be His mouthpiece, and the man this time was Jeremiah.

Jeremiah prophesied through the reigns of five kings, although only three are mentioned in the opening verses of his book, for the other two reigned for only three months each. Although the majority of the nation had turned away from God there were still some who feared the Lord, and Jeremiah belonged to such a family. His father was Hilkiah, who may well have been the high priest who discovered the book of the law in the house of God in the reign of Josiah. A comparison of Jeremiah 32:7 with 2 Chronicles 34:22 suggests that Shallum, the husband of Huldah the prophetess, may have been Jeremiah's uncle. So he was brought up in godly surroundings among people who feared the Lord. He must surely have felt the influence of their lives, and early in his own life he set his heart to serve the Lord. When God is looking for a man to speak His word He looks for one who has become familiar with His voice in the secret place, and I am sure that Jeremiah was such a man. He was young, perhaps in his late teens or early twenties, when the word of God came to him, and this is how he spoke about his experience:

"The word of the LORD came to me, saying, "Before I formed you in the womb I knew you, before you were born I set you apart; I appointed you as a prophet to the nations". 'Ah, Sovereign LORD", I said, "I do not know how to speak; I am only a child" (Jeremiah 1:4-6 NIV).

What a tremendous word to come to a young man. His response shows the deep impact that it had upon him. He was overwhelmed by the solemnity of it. "Ah Sovereign LORD", he said, "I do not know how to speak." He did not say, "I will not speak", but "I do not know how to speak". It was a cry of weakness rather than unwillingness. Indeed even as he protested, he declared his willingness by the very title he used in speaking to God. The Sovereign Jehovah, the mighty God, the eternal Jehovah was his supreme Lord, and Jeremiah had already learned that there was no arguing with Him. He felt utterly unable for the task - overwhelmed by the awesomeness of it - but he was not refusing to obey. God loves men like that: men who feel their deep weakness, but are willing to put their trust in Him. God said a very lovely thing to Jeremiah: "Do not say, "I am only a child". You must go to everyone I send you to and say whatever I command you. Do not be afraid of them, for I am with you and will rescue you (Jeremiah 1:7 NIV).

So his strength for the task lay in the fact that God was sending him, and His enabling in the divine command. That statement contained words which have been a source of strength and encouragement to servants of God in all ages, "Do not be afraid ... for I am with you". These are tremendous words, so simple and yet so profound. I am, the divine title, the ever present Jehovah, and you. I am with you. "Lo, I am with you always" (Matthew 28:20) said our risen Master before He took His leave of His apostles. Down through the centuries God's servants have clung to those words at times when everything else seemed to be falling around them, and pinning their faith on them they have gone forward against fearful odds.

2

MY WORDS IN YOUR MOUTH

Shortly before the Second World War a Bible distributor visited a small town in Poland and gave a Bible to a man who was converted through reading it. Bibles were in short supply, so the new believer passed it on to others with the same glorious effect that they were also drawn to Christ. That process continued until that one Bible had been used in the conversion of two hundred persons.

What a power there is in the Word of God! It "is living, and active, and sharper than any two-edged sword" (Hebrews 4:12). Jeremiah found that to be so, and he was called to a lifetime of speaking God's Word. When God first called him he protested for he felt completely unable for the task. "I cannot speak," he said, "for I am a child" (Jeremiah 1:6). God's answer was to put forth His hand and touch Jeremiah's mouth. "Behold, I have put My words in thy mouth", said God (Jeremiah 1:9). Ah, that is the answer, not only for Jeremiah, but for all who are called upon to speak God's Word. May God save us from the error of speaking our own words and teach us to wait on Him in the secret place until we feel His touch, and He puts His words in our mouths. This is so important, for we are living in a world which is hungry for the authoritative preaching of the Word of God.

Let us consider what God said to Jeremiah about His Word, and how Jeremiah viewed his task of speaking that Word to His people: "See, I have this day set thee over the nations and over the kingdoms, to pluck up and to break down, and to destroy and to overthrow; to build, and to plant (Jeremiah 1:10). That is what God said to him. He was called to a work which would affect not only his own country of Judah, but many of the surrounding great nations. The only instrument Jeremiah would use in this work would he the living Word of God. "Thus saith the LORD" was his message, and those words were constantly on his lips. It was necessary therefore that Jeremiah should have great confidence in God's Word; so the first thing that happened after his appointment was that God asked him what he saw. "I see a rod of an almond tree" he said (Jeremiah 1:11).

The almond tree was the symbol of springtime, for it was the first of the trees to blossom; in fact, it was covered with blossom before its leaves appeared. Translated literally it might have been called 'the awake tree', and the conversation between God and Jeremiah might he paraphrased as follows: "What do you see, Jeremiah? 'I see the rod of an almond tree', he said. You see correctly God said, for I awake to My Word, I am watching to see that My word is fulfilled. Men may despise it, they may refuse to receive it from you, but always remember I am watching over it."

What a comfort that must have been to Jeremiah in the long and difficult years ahead. And what a comfort it is to us also, who are called to work with God's Word today. God says: "For as the rain cometh down and the snow from heaven, and returneth not thither, but watereth the earth, and maketh it bring forth and bud, and giveth seed to the sower and bread to the eater; so shall My word be that goeth forth out of My mouth: it shall not return unto Me void, but it shall accomplish that which I please, and it shall prosper in the thing whereto I sow it" (Isaiah 55:10,11).

There were times when the going was so hard that Jeremiah was tempted to give up. He said: "I am become a laughingstock all the day, every one mocketh me the word of the LORD is made a reproach unto me, and a derision, all the day (Jeremiah 20:7,8). Life must have been tough for him, for not only were the people opposed to receiving God's Word, but they were actively against God's servant. Persecution and imprisonment became his way of life, and all because he faithfully spoke God's Word. But he could not give it up: "If I say, I will not make mention of Him, nor speak any more in His Name, then there is in mine heart as it were a burning fire shut up in my bones, and I am' weary with forbearing, and cannot contain" (Jeremiah 20:9). Many a preacher has had that experience; the word of the Lord burning in his heart like a fire. "Is not My Word like as fire? saith the LORD; and like a hammer that breaketh the rock in pieces? (Jeremiah 23:29).

Reader, have you felt the power of the Word of God in your life? Have you felt it hammering away at your heart until you have been forced to face up to what God is saying to you. That is the way God brings blessing into our lives. God told Jeremiah the Word of God through him would be for breaking down and building up, and so it will be in our lives, breaking down the things that are wrong and building up what is right and true and for the glory of God. Let us have hearts to do what God says to us in His Word, and not be a hearer that forgets, but a doer that works, and we shall be blessed in the doing (James 1:25). Then, as we are obedient to the Word ourselves, let us speak it out to others. Let the preachers give themselves to their preaching. The exhortation that Paul gave to Timothy was: "Preach the Word; be prepared in season and out of season; correct, rebuke and encourage – with great patience and careful instruction" (2 Timothy 4:2 NIV).

We are not all called to the public platform, but we are all responsible to speak God's Word at every opportunity that comes our way. "He that hath My Word, let him speak My Word faithfully" (Jeremiah 23:28). Jeremiah has shown us the way; let us follow his example.

3

FIRST LOVE

God called Jeremiah to be a prophet in the thirteenth year of the reign of king Josiah, who was quite a remarkable king. When he was sixteen years of age he began to seek God, and when he was twenty he campaigned against idolatry in his land (2 Chronicles 34:1-3).

A few years later the book of the law was found in God's house, and the reading of it so affected the king that his reforms became even more thorough (2 Chronicles 34:14,19). There was no doubt about his sincerity, but unfortunately it was not shared by his people. God said about them, "Judah hath not returned unto Me with her whole heart, but feignedly" (Jeremiah 3:10). There was change because Josiah insisted upon it, but it was not a change of heart and that was why Jeremiah's task was so difficult.

But if the people were not speaking from their hearts, God certainly was, judging by some of the things He said through Jeremiah in the second chapter of his prophecy. Of the many questions that God asked perhaps the most striking is found in verse 5: "What unrighteousness have your fathers found in Me, that they are gone far from Me, and have walked after vanity, and are become vain?"

It is remarkable that God should ask such a question. Of course it was calculated to bring them to the point where they acknowledged that there was no fault in God and never could be; then it would only be a tiny step for them to take to realize that the fault must be in them, but they never got that far. Patiently God pleaded with them - oh, how much He loved them - and looking back to the early days of their love for Him He said: "I remember for thee the kindness of thy youth, the love of thine espousals; how thou wentest after Me in the wilderness, in a land that was not sown" (v.2).

How like the Lord that was, to give credit where it was due. He never forgot Israel's first love. They did not follow for what they got out of it. All around them was a barren land, and the going was hard. Obviously it was love for the Lord that drew them. That was true love, that follows out of regard for the Person rather than anything He gives. God took note of that and never forgot it.

The Lord Jesus put a searching question to Peter when He said, "Simon, son of John, lovest thou Me?" It drew from Peter's heart the confession, "Yea, Lord; Thou knowest that I love Thee" (John 21:15). First love is a very precious thing. First love produces first works, but first love can fade. The heart can grow cold. That is what happened in Ephesus, and the Lord was caused to say: "But I have this against thee, that thou didst leave thy first love (Revelation 2:4).

The Lord remembers first love and first works, He never forgets. First love produces holy lives. It did that in Israel's case. "Israel was holiness unto the LORD" (v.3). The God who had called them was a holy God, and love for Him had produced holy lives on their part. Their hearts were true, their love was warm, their lives were pure, and their works were full of zeal. But in Jeremiah's day they had strayed far away, and God was pleading with them to tell Him why they had done so.

God had a complaint against His people; they had been unfaithful. They had turned away from His love to worthless idols and to all the sin and uncleanness that went with idol worship, but although He pleaded with them they refused to return to Him. The heart of God was sorely wounded. "Pass over to the Isles of Kittim and see; and send unto Kedar, and consider diligently; and see if there hath been such a thing. Hath a nation changed their gods, which yet are no gods? but My people have changed their Glory for that which doth not profit (vv. 10,11).

His people had treated Him worse than the nations around Israel had treated their idols. The idol gods never demanded anything of their adherents which conflicted with their sinful desires; they could serve their gods and live as they pleased. Israel could not do that with God, and neither can we. Therein lies the great difference. Israel was holy to the Lord as long as their first love lasted, for the God who saved them was a holy God. "Ye shall be holy; for I am holy" is the divine requirement carried from the Old Testament into the New Testament (1 Peter 1:16). It is binding on us all, and in a world that is full of corruption and lust God calls us to lives that are holy and pure. Let us remember that God is looking for love that comes from a pure heart, a good conscience, and sincere faith (1 Timothy 1:5). "Keep thyself pure" is His word to us all.

"But flee youthful lusts, and follow after righteousness, faith, love, peace, with them that call on the Lord out of a pure heart" (2 Timothy 2:22). The message comes to us all today. Soon our Master will return. Will He find our hearts beating true to Him when He comes?

4

LIVING WATER

Who would choose stagnant water out of a cistern in preference to fresh water from a spring? That is what Israel did, and God tells us about it in Jeremiah chapter 2. It is a story of wounded love. God had loved them with an everlasting love and drawn them with lovingkindness, but they had forsaken Him. Recounting it God said: "For My people have committed two evils; they have forsaken Me the fountain of living waters, and hewed them out cisterns, broken cisterns, that can hold no water" (Jeremiah 2:13).

They turned away from God, the fountain of living water, and dug out for themselves cisterns to gather their own water supply. That would have been folly enough had their own cisterns been able to hold water, but they were not, for they were broken cisterns that very soon ran dry. The world has many cisterns too, from which the Devil invites us to draw. Cisterns of pleasure, of sport, of wealth and fame, but they are all broken cisterns. They seem to satisfy for a little while, but they soon run dry and the soul is left unsatisfied and sad.

On the last and great day of the feast of tabernacles the Lord Jesus stood and cried: "If any man thirst, let him come unto Me, and drink" (John 7:37). It is a message that runs through the Scriptures. Some seven centuries before the Lord Jesus came to live amongst us, Isaiah cried: "Ho, every one that thirsteth, come ye to the waters, and he that hath no money; come ye, buy, and eat; yea, come, buy wine and milk without money and without price (Isaiah 55:1).

And on the very last page of our Bibles is the invitation: "And he that is athirst, let him come: he that will, let him take the water of life freely (Revelation 22:17). God knows our hearts are thirsty. He made us that way. We have been made by Him and for Him, and the thirst of our hearts can only be satisfied in Him. There is no other place where the thirst of human hearts can be quenched. The psalmist said: "They shall be abundantly satisfied, for with Thee is the fountain of life (Psalm 36:8,9).

With that the sons of Korah agreed for they said: "My soul thirsteth for God, for the living God" (Psalm 42:2). Let us take a moment to think again of Israel's great mistake. God said that they committed two sins. They had forsaken Him, that was the first sin. The second was that they had dug out their own cisterns. The heart of God was sad. They had refused His love and had turned away from Him. He likened them to an unfaithful bride, for He had been like a husband to them, but they had spurned His love and had gone after other lovers. And is not that the situation when a believer in the Lord Jesus turns to the world to find his satisfaction? That is why James speaks in such plain language when he says: "Ye adulteresses, know ye not that the friendship of the world is enmity with God? Whosoever therefore would be a friend of the world maketh himself an enemy of God" (James 4:4).

It was the world that crucified our Lord. The world did not know Him: it gave Him the outside place and nailed Him to a Cross. The world is no place for those who have tasted of the Saviour's love. Let us be true to the One who died for us, for He satisfies the longing soul.

And one further point, not only will the Lord satisfy our own hearts. He will also use us to bring the living water to others. He says: "He that believeth on Me, as the Scripture hath said, out of his belly shall flow rivers of living water" (John 7:38). What a wonderful promise, to have the living water flowing out through us to others in all their need.

There are three strong reasons therefore why we must guard our hearts from the lure of the world. Firstly, because all that is in the world is passing away, and its cisterns are broken cisterns that hold no water to satisfy our hearts. Secondly, and this is surely the chief reason, because we are the Lord's; He has bought us purchased us with His blood and we belong to Him. Shall we not be true to the One who has loved us even unto death? Thirdly, what of the thirsty hearts around us in all their need? How shall they hear of Christ unless we tell them? How shall the living water reach them unless God channels it through us?

5

THE KNOWLEDGE OF GOD

"Thus saith the LORD, 'Let not the wise man glory in his wisdom, neither let the mighty man glory in his might, let not the rich man glory in his riches: but let him that glorieth glory in this, that he understandeth, and knoweth Me, that I am the LORD which exercise lovingkindness, judgement, and righteousness, in the earth: for in these things I delight', saith the LORD" (Jeremiah 9:23-24).

If God had written these words today they could not have been more up-to-date. These are the very things that men boast in today, the things that occupy so much of their attention - wisdom, knowledge and education, might and power and the influence that goes with it, riches and wealth and all the material things that wealth can buy. These are the things which dominate the lives of so many people in our twenty-first century world. "What is wrong with them?" you may ask; nothing, as far as they go. Wisdom, strength and riches are all gifts from God, so certainly there is nothing wrong with them. But God says we are not to boast in them - in other words, we are not to set our hearts on them.

There are two simple reasons why we should not do so. The first is that these things are all of limited value and the second, they are all passing away. We cannot take them with us when the time comes for us to leave this world. There are things in life which are far more important than these three things put together, and God names them for us, lovingkindness, judgement and righteousness. These are the things He delights in and which He is working out in our world today. Lovingkindness is God's love in action, stooping down to men in their need. Judgement or justice is the administration of human affairs in equity and truth. Righteousness is that which is absolutely true and straight and devoid of perversity or crookedness. God delights in these things.

Let us pause for a moment to consider what sort of world this would be if these three things prevailed. There would be no wars or fighting, no greed and hatred, no violence and brutality, no oppression of the poor or neglect of the handicapped and elderly. We can understand why God delights in these things. Honest men and women are striving after them, but they elude us, and will continue to do so until the Lord Jesus comes and sets up His kingdom. Then, and only then, will there be kindness and justice and righteousness in the earth. These things are in the nature of God; they belong to Him. God is Love, and righteousness and judgement are the foundation of His throne (Psalm 97:2), so if we want them, we will find them in Him. That is why God says - and this is the very kernel of His message - "Let him that glorieth glory in this, that he understandeth, and knoweth Me". The knowledge of God is the most precious thing in all the world. The Lord Jesus said: "And this is Life eternal, that they should know Thee the only true God, and Him whom Thou didst send, even Jesus Christ" (John 17:3).

There is absolutely nothing that can compare with the knowledge of God. Let not a man boast in his wisdom, but let him get to know God who is all-wise. All the treasures of wisdom and knowledge are hidden in Jesus Christ (Colossians 2:3); let not a man boast in his strength or might, but in God who is almighty. He has decreed that the government of the world shall be on the shoulder of His beloved Son. Let not a man boast in his riches, but let him boast in the Lord who is all-sufficient not only in riches, but in all things. Soon God will display to a wondering world that all riches and honour belong to His Son.

Let us get the message for it is such an important one; the omniscient, omnipotent, all-sufficient God will one day right all earth's wrongs, and He will do it during a thousand years of perfect peace, when His Son will reign to earth's fullest extent, and the knowledge of God will cover the earth as the waters cover the sea (Isaiah 11:1-9). The knowledge of the Lord must be the supreme quest of our lives. The apostle Paul had this objective before him. He had many things to his credit humanly speaking, many things that men would count as gain. But he knew what was of eternal value and he said: "Howbeit what things were gain to me, these have I counted loss for Christ. Yea verily. and I count all things to be loss for the excellency of the knowledge of Christ Jesus my Lord (Philippians 3:7,8). May God help each one of us to learn from Paul's example.

6

THE POTTER'S HOUSE

It is fascinating to watch a craftsman at work, to see something of beauty and usefulness taking shape under his hands as he skilfully uses his tools. It was to such an experience that God called Jeremiah when He said: "Arise, and go down to the potter's house, and there I will cause thee to hear My words. Then I went down to the potter's house, and, behold, he wrought his work on the wheels" (Jeremiah 18:2,3).

We can picture the scene as Jeremiah stood in the potter's house and watched him at his work, but it was not merely a question of interest; God had a lesson for him to learn from the potter and it is one which applies to us also. A key text in Isaiah helps us to understand the point that is being made. The prophet says: "But now, O LORD, Thou art our Father; we are the clay, and Thou our Potter; and we all are the work of Thy hand (Isaiah 64:8).

God is the Potter and we are the clay, and He is working in our lives, if we allow Him, to make us into vessels that He can use in His service and for His glory. Paul describes it to Timothy: "A vessel unto honour, sanctified, meet for the Master's use, prepared unto every good work (2

Timothy 2:21).

With these verses in mind let us consider the message God had for Jeremiah and learn the lesson of the potter's house. We would agree at the beginning that before the potter commences his work he has a plan in mind. He can see in his mind's eye the vessel he is about to make. And God has a plan in His mind as He works in our lives. In Jeremiah chapter 29 He states this clearly: "For I know the plans I have for you," declares the LORD, "plans to prosper you and not to harm you, plans to give you hope and a future" (v.11 NIV). That is a particularly precious verse. If we link it with Ephesians 2:10 we can see that God had a plan in mind long before He started working on us, for there Paul says: "For we are His workmanship, created in Christ Jesus for good works, which God afore prepared that we should walk in them."

It is wonderful to realize that before we were born God had His plan for us, and now that we are saved He is working out that plan in our lives, or at least He wants to if we will allow Him. His plan for each one of us is different. He does not make two vessels alike. If each blade of grass is different, and no two snowflakes are exactly alike, we can be perfectly sure that when God works in human lives He produces in each one of us His own unique work of art. What a wonderful contemplation!

God is at work in our lives to produce in us something for His glory and usefulness - vessels suitable for our heavenly Father's use. But how does He do it? Ah, we must watch the potter at his work to see that two things are involved. There is the turning of the wheel and the skilful hands of the potter. The potter places the lump of soft clay on the revolving wheel and then under his hands the vessel takes shape. The turning wheel and the skilful hands produce the desired result. Is that not the way the divine Potter deals with us? On the wheel of life He works; in the continuous round of daily experience His hands are upon us, applying a little pressure here and a little pressure there until He shapes us into a vessel that He can use.

But we have to be willing to respond to the pressure of His hands. The pressure takes different forms, of course; sometimes it comes in the discipline that is referred to in Hebrews chapter 12, and the secret of benefiting from such discipline is to be exercised by it, to accept it as God's training for us. The apostle Paul sums it all up when he asks, "Hath not the potter a right over the clay?" (Romans 9:21). That question goes to the heart of the matter.

> Have Thine own way, Lord,
> Have Thine own way;
> Thou art the Potter
> I am the clay
> Mould me and make me
> After Thy will,
> While I am waiting,
> Yielded and still.
>
> Have Thine own way, Lord
> Have Thine own way;
> Hold o'er my being absolute sway.
> Fill with Thy Spirit
> Till all shall see
> Christ only, always,
> Living in me.
> (A.A. Pollard)

When we can say that and mean it sincerely, then the divine Potter is able to work out His plan in our lives. While Jeremiah was in the potter's house he saw the vessel that was made marred in the hand of the potter, and he watched the potter forming it again into another vessel, shaping it as seemed best to him. Is not that a tremendous word when we apply it to ourselves? The divine Potter wants to shape our lives as seems best to Him, and we can be sure that what is best to Him is the very best for us. Sometimes through our failure, our unwillingness to yield to His hand, the vessel is marred. It was so in Peter's case. He chose his own way and ended up denying his Master with oaths and curses. But he wept his way back with bitter tears of repentance, and the divine Potter began again in His love and patience and formed dear Peter into a very useful vessel. He became one of God's most useful and valuable servants.

Perhaps you, too, have failed. Do not be unduly discouraged. Confess your failure, and ask the Lord to begin again with you, and assuredly He will. We only require a deep love in our hearts for the Lord and a sincere desire for His plan to be worked out in our lives and He will ensure that it is. Let us remember that He is the Potter and we are just the clay. Let us be pliable in His hands, and accept the pressures He applies as part of His perfect plan, and He will mould us and make us after His will.

7

THE NEW COVENANT

Very often God reserves His brightest promises for the darkest days. It was so in the case of the promise God spoke through Jeremiah when the Babylonian army was mustering outside the city of Jerusalem, ready to destroy it and to carry its people away into captivity because of their repeated disobedience.

The outlook could hardly have been darker, and it was then that God gave them, like a shaft of light, His most wonderful promise. Here it is: "Behold, the days come, saith the LORD, that I will make a new covenant with the house of Israel, and with the house of Judah: not according to the covenant that I made with their fathers in the day that I took them by the hand to bring them out of the land of Egypt; But this is the covenant that I will make ... I will put My law in their inward parts, and in their heart will I write it; and I will be their God, and they shall be My people: and they shall teach no more every man his neighbour, and every man his brother, saying, Know the LORD: for they shall all know Me, from the least of them unto the greatest of them, saith the LORD: for I will forgive their iniquity, and their sin will I remember no more" (Jeremiah 31:31-34).

These are remarkable words, and they are quoted in full in Hebrews chapter 8, for the day is coming when God will completely fulfil this promise and take up Israel once again as His people. So many portions of the Word of God speak of those great days that are coming for Israel. But that is not all, for if you turn over to chapter 10 of Hebrews you will find that this same promise has its application to us today: "And the Holy Spirit also beareth witness to us: for after He hath said, 'This is the covenant that I will make with them … then saith He, and their sins and their iniquities will I remember no more'" (vv. 15-17).

These are great words and they are written to us, as the Holy Spirit bears witness. It is possible for us to be linked with God in this covenant relationship which has various aspects. In Hebrews chapter 9 we read, "Now even the first covenant had ordinances of divine service" (v.1), and if the first covenant had them, so has the new covenant which embraces us. This service with its ordinances belongs to God's house where His people serve Him according to the pattern set out in His Word.

Let us think about the terms of the covenant, taking them in reverse order and beginning where we must all begin in our relationship with God, with the work of Christ in putting away sin by the sacrifice of Himself. The scripture says: For by one offering He hath perfected for ever them that are sanctified (Hebrews 10:14). It is on account of that one sacrifice that God says "their sins and their iniquities will I remember no more" and "as far as the east is from the west, so far hath He removed our transgressions from us" (Psalm 103:12). That is a glorious truth, and it applies to all believers in the Lord Jesus Christ. The second of the terms of the covenant concerns the knowledge of God.

"For all shall know Me, from the least to the greatest of them" (Hebrews 8:11).

"And this is life eternal, that they should know Thee the only true God, and Him whom Thou didst send, even Jesus Christ" (John 17:3).

There is nothing in the world to compare with this knowledge. The third term of the covenant, the one that is put first in the order in which God gives them to us, relates to putting His laws in our minds and writing them on our hearts, so that we may serve Him intelligently with our minds and lovingly from our hearts. This truth touches you and me today.

Are we willing to let God by His Spirit write His laws on our minds and hearts? Paul speaks of the Word of God being written on the fleshy tablets of our hearts in contrast to the law that was written on tablets of stone. Writing to the Church of God in the city of Corinth he said: "Ye are our epistle, written in our hearts, known and read of all men; being made manifest that ye are an epistle of Christ, ministered by us, written not with ink, but with the Spirit of the living God; not in tables of stone, but in tables that are hearts of flesh (2 Corinthians 3:2,3).

A church of God is a precious place in which to be. It is a company of disciples in a town or city on whose hearts Christ has written His Word by the operation of the Holy Spirit, and this has resulted in their being gathered together to obey that Word in fellowship with the people of God. They are seeking to put it into practice in the way they live, and in the way they serve God together. Are we willing to let Him write His Word and His will deeply in our hearts? We can see what will be involved if we do. It will mean that we no longer live to please ourselves, but to please the One who has brought us into covenant with Himself. But that is the great purpose for which God has saved us, and through us Christ will be sending out His message to men and women around us. We shall be like a letter from Christ that all men may read.

8

THE FIELD IN ANANOTH

"How can I be sure of God's will in the big decisions of life?" That is a question that is often asked. Every one of us who loves the Lord Jesus wants to be sure that we are doing what pleases Him when it comes to making decisions which will affect the whole course of our lives. But how can we be sure?

There is an incident in the life of Jeremiah which helps us on this point. It is found in Jeremiah chapter 32. Jeremiah was shut up in prison at the time, for king Zedekiah did not like the message that he was bringing from the Lord. For forty years Jeremiah had been warning Judah of God's coming judgement on account of their sin, and now his words were coming to pass, for the army of Babylon was surrounding Jerusalem, and the people could not get in or out.

At that very point in time, when the overthrow of the city was imminent, God spoke to Jeremiah and told him to buy a field in his home town of Anathoth. Jeremiah was greatly perplexed. God had said that they were going into captivity for seventy years; surely it was no time for buying a field. Was it really God who was speaking to him, or had he been

26

mistaken? That was the question. Jeremiah was not sure. Sometimes we are brought into situations where we are faced with big decisions and we are not sure which way to go.

In Jeremiah's case he was given clear guidance by God, for a short time after God had spoken to him his uncle's son came to him with the proposal that he buy the field just as God said he should. Then Jeremiah knew that the word was indeed from the Lord, the circumstances had confirmed it. Is not that often the case in our own experience? When the following four things work together we may be fairly sure that God is leading us on. Firstly, there is the inclination of the heart brought about, either by some word from God through the Scriptures, or by some urge that the Holy Spirit brings. Secondly, as we pray about it circumstances appear to tie in.

Thirdly, and this is important, we seek the advice of other Christian friends, those who have passed through life's experiences with the Lord, and whose advice we can trust. It is important to share with others the big decisions of life, and be guided by their counsel, rather than go it alone. During all the time we arc considering the matter we should continue to make it the subject of our daily prayers. Fourthly, and finally, in response to prayer there comes an answer of peace to the heart. If there is a sincere desire on our part to take God's way and not our own way He will surely not allow us to make any serious mistakes if we follow these steps.

When Jeremiah was assured that God had spoken he did not hesitate for a moment. He did not understand why he was being asked to buy property, for it seemed to be a strange time for such a transaction. But once he was sure that it was of God, he subscribed the deed in the presence of witnesses, paid the money, and asked Baruch to put both copies of the deed in an earthen vessel where they would be preserved until such time as God brought the Jews back to their own land. The transaction was a confirmation to all who witnessed it that God's Word would come to pass and after seventy years had run their course God would bring His people back to their own land.

Jeremiah knew all that, but he was still puzzled. Why had God asked him to buy land at that particular time? So, after he had obeyed and put the deed into safe custody he prayed. It is important to notice the sequence of events. He obeyed first and then he brought his query to the Lord in the lovely prayer that is recorded in chapter 32 (vv. 17–25). It is really an outstanding prayer, showing his strong faith in God, a confidence which had been built up over many years through many experiences with God: "Ah Lord GOD! behold, Thou hast made the heaven and the earth by Thy great power and by Thy stretched out arm; there is nothing too hard for Thee" (v.17).

It was with these words that Jeremiah began his prayer, then at the close of it he spoke of his problem: "Behold ... the city is given into the hands of the Chaldeans ... and what Thou hast spoken is come to pass ... and Thou hast said ... buy thee the field for money (vv. 24,25).

God came back to Jeremiah with His answer: "Behold, I am the LORD, the God of all flesh: is there any thing too hard for Me?" (v.27). He used Jeremiah's own words. It was as if He was saying to Jeremiah, "these are your own words, but do you really believe them? Do they apply in every circumstance, and even in this matter of the buying of the field?" You may remember that God asked the same question once before in Genesis chapter 18.

He promised Abraham and Sarah a son in their old age, and Sarah laughed in unbelief, and the Lord said to Abraham, "Is any thing too hard for the LORD? (v.14). It was through the seed promised to Abraham that God was going to bring into the world His own dear Son, through whom all His purposes would be accomplished. There is nothing too hard for God; He works all things after the counsel of His will. Let us go forward in faith as Jeremiah did, in the strong confidence that to the God we love and serve nothing is impossible. There is nothing too hard for Him!

9

THE RECHABITES

We read about the Rechabites in Jeremiah chapter 35. Their history goes far back into the Old Testament, for Rechab their progenitor belonged to the Kenites who threw in their lot with Israel, being related to Moses through marriage (Judges 1:16).

But the man who made them famous was called Jonadab. Jonadab showed his zeal for God when he joined with Jehu in the campaign against the wicked house of Ahab and the worship of Baal. Jonadab gave commandment to his sons and daughters that they should drink no wine, build no houses, but live in tents, sow no seed and plant no vineyards. His instructions seemed to be very severe, and we might argue that he was depriving them of perfectly legitimate things.

However, it is obvious that he was a man who feared God deeply, and seeing the awful wickedness around him he desired to preserve his posterity from such sin and lawlessness, and so he placed them under this solemn pledge. It was calculated to preserve their pilgrim character and keep them from putting down roots. The great founders of the nation of Israel had been pilgrims who lived in tents, and Jonadab decided that his family should do the same. The remarkable thing is that 250 years later his descendants were absolutely true to this family tradition, and that is what it was. A tradition is something handed down from one generation to another, and from one generation to another they had passed it on and had lived by it: So firmly did they adhere to the family tradition that when Jeremiah tried to persuade them to drink wine they flatly refused, and out came the story of the commandment of Jonadab their father.

We have obeyed the voice of Jonadab the son of Rechab our father in all that he charged us, to drink no wine all our days, we, our wives, our sons, nor our daughters; nor to build houses for us to dwell in: neither have we vineyard, nor field, nor seed: but we have dwelt in tents, and have obeyed, and done according to all that Jonadab our father commanded us" (Jeremiah 35:8-10). Jeremiah did not want to tempt the Rechabites into disloyalty to their pledge; he wanted to use the example of their devotion as an object lesson for God's people, Judah. The Rechabites had been far more true to the commandments of their forefathers than Judah had been to the commandments of the Lord. That is the main point that comes out of the story to provide a lesson for us today.

Let us think for a moment about the power of tradition. You may have your own thoughts about the demands that Jonadab placed on his family and whether he was asking more than was reasonable, but perhaps you will agree that if the demands kept them from sin and resulted in a closer walk with God there was profit in them. They also illustrate the amazing power of tradition, for after some 250 years Jonadab's descendants were still keeping strictly to the details of his instructions. There is no doubt that men love to be loyal to tradition. Is that a good thing or a bad thing? It depends on whether or not the traditions are according to God's Word. The Lord Jesus had stern words for the Pharisees about their traditions because they cut right across the clear commandments of God. He said: "Ye have made void the Word of God because of your tradition (Matthew 15:6).

On the other hand there were traditions which the apostles urged the disciples to keep because they were based on God's Word. Paul, writing to the Church of God in Corinth, commended them for their observance of such traditions: "Now I praise you that ye remember me in all things, and hold fast the traditions, even as I delivered them unto you" (1 Corinthians 11:2).

So this is a point of real interest to us all, for tradition dies hard as we have seen. Are you and I bound by any tradition in our family lives or in our church associations? That is a question worth asking ourselves, and if we are, let us check them out with God's Word to make sure that they are not cutting across any plain commandment of the Lord.

Let us now think about the other lesson that comes out of the passage we are considering. It is the lesson that Jeremiah so much wanted his people to learn, and that is why he offered the Rechabites wine to drink. God wanted their loyalty to family tradition to be an object lesson to His people.

"Then came the word of the LORD unto Jeremiah, saying, Thus saith the LORD of hosts, the God of Israel; Go, and say to the men of Judah and the inhabitants of Jerusalem, Will ye not receive instruction to hearken to My words? said the LORD. The words of Jonadab the son of Rechab, that he commanded his sons, not to drink wine, are performed, and unto this day they drink none, for they obey their father's commandment: but I have spoken unto you, rising up early and speaking; and ye have not hearkened unto Me" (vv. 12-14).

These are solemn words. You can almost feel the heart of God yearning after His people. He further says: "I have sent also unto you all My servants the prophets ... saying, 'Return ye now every man from his evil way, and amend your doings' ... but ye have not ... hearkened unto Me" (v.15).

God is speaking to us also, speaking through His Word. Are we paying attention? So much depends upon our response to His Word. God longs to bless us, but He can only do so in the rich and full way He desires if we are obedient to Him. Let us make sure that our hearts are sensitive to His Word, and that we are careful to obey even in the small details of what He says. It was a young boy who said to God, "Speak; for Thy servant heareth" (1 Samuel 3:10). Let us follow that good example.

> Master, speak Thy servant heareth,
> Waiting for Thy gracious word,
> Longing for the voice that cheereth;
> Master, let it now be heard.
> I am listening, Lord, for Thee,
> What hast Thou to say to me?
>
> Master, speak and make me ready,
> When Thy voice is truly heard,
> With obedience glad and steady
> Still to follow every word;
> I am listening, Lord, for Thee,
> What hast Thou to say to me?
> (F.R. Havergal)

10

GOD'S SUFFERING SERVANT

What would you do with old rags and worn-out clothes? Most people would throw them away as useless, but Ebed-melech the Ethiopian found a use for them. The story of how he made use of such material is found in chapter 38 of the book of Jeremiah. Jeremiah was cast into a dungeon by the princes of Judah, and he sank in the mire to the bottom of the dungeon. The princes wanted to put him to death because God's message which he had been speaking was not acceptable to them. There is little doubt that he would have died in that miry pit had God not intervened and sent Ebed-melech the kind Ethiopian to his help.

Ebed-melech went boldly to the king and told him of Jeremiah's plight and received his permission and the help of thirty men to lift the prophet out of the dungeon. It is the way that he went about the rescue that is appealing. The matter was urgent, and he might well have reasoned that the only thing that mattered was to haul Jeremiah out of that pit as quickly as possible, regardless of how painful it might be for him. Ebed-melech, however, was a kindly man who had a careful thought for others, and snatching up some old rags and worn out clothes he took them with him. When he reached the pit he lowered them down to Jeremiah telling him to put them under his arms to pad the ropes, and so the dear man was lifted out of his prison with the minimum of discomfort.

Thank God for Ebed-melech and his old rags. We should always feel thankful that God has included details like this in His holy Word, for there is a lesson for us to learn from them. "Be ye kind one to another", the scripture says (Ephesians 4:32). It is a lovely thing when Christians go out of their way to show such kindnesses, not only to fellow Christians, but to all persons who touch their lives. There is surely no more effective way of presenting Christ to a world lost in sin than by such little acts of kindness. "Actions speak louder than words" someone has said, and very often they do.

The foregoing comments are, however, by way of introduction for the main purpose in drawing attention to this episode in Jeremiah's life is to show how typical he was of the Lord Jesus as God's suffering Servant. There are so many similarities between Jeremiah and the Lord Jesus. Both could be described as "a man of sorrows, and acquainted with grief' (Isaiah 53:3). Both of them wept over Jerusalem because of the unwillingness of the people to hear God's Word. It was written of the Lord Jesus that "He came unto His own, and they that were His own received Him not" (John 1:11), and the same was true of Jeremiah. Both of them were rejected, and both suffered at the hands of men. Jeremiah was beaten before being cast into prison, and we are reminded how the Lord Jesus was stripped and beaten and eventually led out to Calvary.

By nature Jeremiah was a very sensitive man, and not one to whom public speaking came easily. When God called him he said, "I cannot speak: for I am a child" (Jeremiah 1:6). He was not the sort of man that one would have expected God to call to such a hard task, but God strengthened him specially for it. In fact God said to him: "Behold, I have made thee this day a fenced city, and an iron pillar, and brasen walls, against the whole land (Jeremiah 1:18).

For over forty years he stood boldly for God against princes, prophets, priests and the people, and he never wavered. How like the Lord Jesus he was in all this. Psalm 80 refers to the Lord as "the Son of Man whom Thou madest strong for Thyself" (v.17). There is no doubt God intends that when we read about Jeremiah we should be reminded of the Lord Jesus as God's suffering Servant. Psalm 69 is a Messianic psalm, and we all think of the sufferings of the Lord Jesus when we read its words: "Save Me, O God; for the waters are come in unto My soul. I sink in deep mire, where there is no standing: I 'am come into deep waters, where the floods overflow Me. Deliver Me out of the mire, and let Me not sink: let Me be delivered from them that hate Me, and out of the deep waters" (vv. 1,2,14).

When we link these words with those of Jeremiah chapter 38, and think about God's servant sinking in the mire in that deep dungeon, we can see how vividly he portrays the Lord Jesus as the suffering Servant. Jeremiah had been called to suffer as well as to serve, and so were all God's servants. God said about Saul of Tarsus the day he was saved on the road to Damascus, "I will shew him how many things he must suffer for My name's sake" (Acts 9:16). But he was no exception, great servant though he was. The early Christians were all called to suffer. To the Philippians Paul wrote: "Because to you it hath been granted in the behalf of Christ, not only to believe on Him, but also to suffer in His behalf (Philippians 1:29).

We leave the thought with you for your meditation that if we are going to follow where Christ leads the way, there will be suffering involved. The Saviour said: "If any man would come after Me, let him deny himself and take up his cross daily, and follow Me" (Luke 9:23).

Can you think of taking up a cross without some measure of suffering? But the pathway of suffering brings its own compensations, for the Master went on to say: "Whosoever would save his life shall lose it; but whosoever shall lose his life for My sake, the same shall save it" (Luke 9:24). He stated a principle in those words which He repeated on a number of occasions. If we are willing to lose for His sake, we will gain in the life to come. So by faith we look ahead to another day that is coming when suffering will give place to glory. We shall be so glad in that day that we joined the ranks pf those who follow a suffering Master, and that we have not shrunk from taking our cross and following Him.

> Measure thy life by loss instead of gain,
> Not by the wine drunk, but by the wine poured forth;
> For love's strength standeth in love's sacrifice,
> And whoso suffers most, hath most to give.

11

BURNING THE ROLL

Have you ever read the story of how we got our English Bible? It is an enthralling story of men who gave all that they had, and even life itself - to bring the Word of God to us in our own mother tongue.

William Tyndale was perhaps the foremost of the pioneers, and one day he said to the local clergy, "If God give me life, 'ere many years the ploughboys shall know more of the Scriptures than you do". And that is just what he did, but it cost him his life to do it. The invention of the printing machine greatly helped him, of course, but the opposition to his work was almost unbelievable. At one time his antagonists bought every copy of the Scriptures that they could find and burned them at St: Paul's. But God can make the wrath of man to praise Him, and with the money received, Tyndale was able to publish copies of the Scriptures more cheaply and in clearer print, and so the Word of God prevailed. It must do, of course, for it is God's living Word, and He plainly says, "the Word of the Lord abideth forever" (1 Peter 1:25).

Burning copies of God's Word was not new, for we read in Jeremiah chapter 36 that king Jehoiakim did the very same thing. God spoke His words to Jeremiah, and Baruch his scribe wrote it down on a roll as Jeremiah dictated it to him. Then Jeremiah told Baruch to go and stand at a busy thoroughfare leading to God's house and read the words to the people as they passed by. This was done at an especially busy time in Jerusalem, a day of a Fast, and crowds of people heard the words God had spoken through Jeremiah. Among those who heard them was a young man called Micaiah, and he passed the word to the princes, who were so concerned about the judgement Jeremiah predicted that they reported the words to the king. Jehoiakim, the king, was not satisfied in hearing about it by word of mouth; he commanded them to bring the roll and read it to him. It was winter time, and he was sitting in his winter house warming himself before a fire.

It is a vivid picture that the scripture presents to us of the godless king surrounded by his princes, all with solemn faces because of the seriousness of the words they were hearing. The king was renowned for his angry outbursts, and as he listened to the words being read he became visibly enraged. Snatching his knife he hacked through three or four columns of the roll and threw them into the fire. Three of his princes were horrified and tried to persuade him not to do it, but he just continued in his anger until the whole of the roll was destroyed. And the scripture says that they were not afraid, neither the king nor any of his servants.

Foolish king! Did he think that he could do away with God's Word as easily as that? If he did he was terribly mistaken. The Lord Jesus said, "Heaven and earth shall pass away, but My words shall not pass away" (Matthew 24:35), and that applies to all of God's Word. Men may destroy copies of it, but the living Word itself can never be destroyed. God told Jeremiah to write again on another roll all the former words and to them were added pronouncements of judgement on Jehoiakim which in due course were fulfilled.

Men are still bent on destroying God's Word, not burning it now, at any rate not often, but in more sophisticated ways they are destroying it. Today we frequently find men and women taking it upon themselves to criticize God's Word; they hack away large portions of it by casting doubt on its truthfulness. Have nothing to do with such error. Stand firmly and bravely, if need be, for the truth of God's Word in its entirety, for the whole of it is divinely inspired. Men have been attacking it for centuries, but it stands firm like a rock. A poet has written:

> Last eve I passed beside the blacksmith's door
> And heard the anvil ring the vesper chime;
> When looking down, I saw upon the floor
> Old hammers worn with use in former time.
> "How many anvils have you used" said I,
> "To wear and batter all these hammers so?"
> "Just one!" said he, and then, with twinkling eye,
> "The anvil wears the hammers out, you know".
> Just so, thought I, the anvil of God's Word
> For ages sceptic blows have beat upon;
> Yet, though the noise of falling blows was heard,
> The anvil is unharmed - the hammers gone.
> (Source unknown)

How very true. No harm can come to the Word of God; it is safe in God's keeping, but great harm comes to those who refuse its words. Jehoiakim found that to his cost, and so will all those who refuse to receive God's Word into their hearts. The Lord Jesus spoke very solemn words when He said: "He that rejecteth Me, and receiveth not My sayings, hath one that judgeth him: the word that I spake, the same shall judge him in the last day" (John 12:48).

One final point. Is it not a remarkable thing that fathers and sons so often stand in contrast to one another? Jehoiakim had a father called Josiah, and he was a king who loved God and deeply reverenced God's Word. In fact it was during his reign that Hilkiah found the book of the law in God's house. It had been lost for a long time, and amazingly enough, lost in God's house. When it was found and read to the king he humbled himself and wept because of the disobedience of his people. What a difference! Two men, a father and a son, but poles apart in their attitude to God's Word. God says, "to this man will I look", or as the New International Version puts it, "This is the one I esteem: he who is humble and contrite in spirit, and trembles at My Word" (Isaiah 66:2). Let us be among those who have such reverence for God's Word that we tremble at the prospect of disobeying it.

12

ZEDEKIAH

A young boy, the son of a missionary in Africa, was playing in the garden of their mission home, when suddenly he heard his father's voice calling from the verandah. "Philip! obey me instantly. Drop to the ground!" The lad did as he was told without any question, for the tone of his father's voice was so urgent. "Now crawl toward me as fast as you can". Again the boy obeyed. "Now stand up and run". He did, and only when he landed in his father's arms did he learn the reason for the urgent instructions. Looking back he saw, hanging from the tree under which he had been playing, a dangerous snake that was fifteen feet long. What a good thing that he had not argued or even hesitated. His life had depended upon his instant obedience.

Our spiritual life and progress depends upon our obedience to the Word of God. We can hardly over emphasize the importance of such obedience, for it is written on almost every page of our Bibles.

Zedekiah was the last of Judah's kings. During his reign the people were carried into captivity, and he among them. He was a weak sort of man ruled by his princes rather than ruling himself. One time when his princes requested that Jeremiah should be put to death, he replied, "Behold, he is in your hand: for the king is not he that can do any thing against you" (Jeremiah 38:5). But weak as he was he understood the value of God's Word, and deep in his heart he respected God's prophet. One day in his distress he sent secretly for Jeremiah, who was then in prison, and asked, "Is there any word from the LORD?" And the answer was "There is" (Jeremiah 37:17). At another secret meeting Jeremiah pleaded with him: "Obey, I beseech thee, the voice of the LORD, in that which I speak unto thee: so shall it be well with thee, and thy soul shall live" (Jeremiah 38:20).

This is where Zedekiah failed; he wanted to know what God had to say, he valued His Word to that extent, but he was not prepared to obey it. What God asked him to do cut across his own desires, and he chose his own way rather than God's. The last picture that we have of him is pathetic. He was taken captive by Nebuchadnezzar the Babylonian king; his sons were put to death before his eyes, then his eyes were put out and he was bound in fetters and carried into Babylon. What a fearful penalty to pay for disobedience. God has put that sad story on the page of His Word so that we shall be warned by it.

In Jeremiah chapter 17 we read these words: "Blessed is the man that trusteth in the LORD, and whose hope the LORD is. For he shall be as a tree planted by the waters, and that spreadeth out his roots by the river, and shall not fear when the heat cometh, but his leaf shall be green; and shall not be careful in the year of drought, neither shall cease from yielding fruit" (vv. 7,8).

Then God immediately goes on to say: "The heart is deceitful above all things, and it is desperately sick: who can know it?" (v.9). Our own hearts are not to be trusted, for they are deceitful; they will lead us astray, but we can trust the Lord. His Word is absolutely true, and what He says is always for our highest good. Why are we so slow sometimes to trust Him? "Trust in the LORD with all thine heart, and lean not upon thine own understanding: in all thy ways acknowledge Him, and He shall direct thy paths" (Proverbs 3:5,6).

Who could wish for a finer promise than that, and yet sometimes we still go our own way. "Is there any word from the LORD?" Yes, there is, there always is, for God in His mercy is still speaking. But have we ears to hear, and hearing shall we obey? Of the believers in Rome it is recorded that they became obedient from the heart to the teaching they were given from the Word of God. The Greek word (hupakoe) translated "obedience" in the New Testament is an interesting one. It comes from two Greek words ('hupo': under, 'akouo': to hear) and it conveys the thought of placing ourselves under what we hear. That is just what Zedekiah failed to do, and the result was tragic. Let us learn the lesson that the results of such recorded failures would teach us, and be obedient from our hearts to what God is saying to us in His Word.

The Bible tells us: "through the one man's disobedience the many were made sinners" (Romans 5:19). That one man was Adam, and all the trouble in our world started through his disobedience. But thank God for the next part of the verse, "Even so through the obedience of the One shall the many be made righteous". The Lord Jesus came to put right the havoc sin had wrought, and He did that by obedience to His Father's will. His obedience opened up the way back to God for every sinner who believes in Him. We are saved by the simple response of obedience to the gospel invitation, and by continuing obedience to God's Word we enter into the blessings He has planned for us. Jeremiah's message to the king holds good for us today. "Obey ... the voice of the LORD. ... so shall it be well with thee."

II

12 PICTURES OF CHRIST IN GENESIS

13

12 PICTURES OF CHRIST IN GENESIS

1) IN THE BEGINNING GOD

"In the beginning God." In this majestic way the canon of Scripture opens. They are just simple words in our English language, but placed together by inspiration of the Holy Spirit they convey profound truth to our hearts. "In the beginning God." As far back as human minds can go, and further still, God was always there. "Even from everlasting to everlasting, Thou art God", said Moses in the lovely 90th psalm.

Think about these words as they apply to our Lord Jesus, for He speaks of Himself in the final chapter of Revelation, "I am the Alpha and the Omega, the First and the Last, the Beginning and the End". As the Father is, so is He. He is the beginning of all creation. "All things were made by Him, and without Him was not anything made that hath been made". He is the Firstborn of all creation, in the sense that He has priority and precedence above all created beings and things. He is the pre-eminent One, for it was the good pleasure of the Father that in Him should all the

47

fulness dwell.

He is the beginning of God's ways, the One in whom all the treasures of wisdom and knowledge are hidden. "Doth not wisdom cry?" asks king Solomon in the first verse of Proverbs chapter 8, and then he goes on to describe Wisdom personified in God's only Son. "The Lord possessed Me in the beginning of His ways". I love the way Cowper has put it in his poem:

> Ere God had built the mountains,
> Or raised the fruitful hills;
> Before He filled the fountains
> That feed the running rills;
> In One from everlasting,
> The wonderful I AM,
> Found pleasures never wasting,
> And Wisdom was His name.
>
> When, like a tent to dwell in,
> He spread the skies abroad,
> And swathed about the swelling
> Of ocean's mighty flood,
> He wrought by weight and measure;
> Wisdom was with Him then;
> Himself the Father's pleasure,
> And His the sons of men.

He is the beginning of divine revelation. "In the beginning was the Word, and the Word was with God, and the Word was God"! He is the One through whom God has chosen to express Himself. Having of old time spoken to the fathers in the prophets, He has at the end of these days spoken unto us in His Son. John looked into a future day and he saw the heaven opened and the Lord Jesus coming forth to judge and make war, and His name is called the Word of God.

2) THE CREATOR

In the evening of the day when the Lord Jesus was raised from the dead, two of His followers were walking from Jerusalem to Emmaus. Very sad and disconsolate they were, for their Master had been crucified and buried in a tomb and all their hopes for Him had been shattered. They were talking together about all that had happened, when a Stranger joined them and walked with them. They did not realize who He was until later when they had invited Him into their home and He was revealed to them as He took the bread and gave thanks for it and gave it to them. Then they knew Him and understood how He had thrilled their hearts as He opened the Scriptures to them. Beginning from Moses and all the prophets He interpreted to them in all the Scriptures the things concerning Himself. The books of Moses, of course, are the first five books of our Bible, perhaps the part most under attack by those who take it upon themselves to criticize God's Word. But to those of us who love our Lord Jesus, these books are just full of Himself.

In the very first verse He is present, for it says, "In the beginning God created the heaven and the earth". Hebrew scholars tell us that while God is a plural noun, the verb "created" is in the singular. Certainly the Holy Spirit was there, for the next verse says "the Spirit of God moved upon the face of the waters". And so was the Lord Jesus, for the apostle John tells us that all things were made by Him; and without Him was not anything made that hath been made.

In the Genesis account we read, "And' God said, Let there be light: and there was light". It was a word of almighty power. "He spake, and it was done", said the psalmist, "He commanded, and it stood fast" (Psalm 33:9). And with that agrees the word in Hebrews chapter 11, "By faith we understand that the worlds have been framed by the Word of God". It was the Eternal Word who spoke in creative power. "In the beginning was the Word, and the Word was with God, and the Word was God". That is one of His glorious titles which He will keep forever. By Him the worlds were brought into being, working together with His Father and the Holy Spirit. He is the great Creator God. Such were some of the great things those two disciples learnt on that unforgettable walk to Emmaus.

3) THE CHURCH THE BODY

The Scriptures are full of Christ, and when we love our Lord Jesus it is exciting to find Him on every page of our Bibles. "Ye search the Scriptures" He said to the Jews who did not believe on Him, "because ye think that in them ye have eternal life; and these are they which bear witness of Me". They failed to find Him in the Scriptures because their hearts were darkened by sin, but when the eyes of our hearts are enlightened Christ shines on every page!

In Genesis chapter 2 there is an arresting word. "The LORD God said, it is not good that the man should be alone; I will make him an help meet for him". Everything else in His creation was good and each day He pronounced it so. On the final day "God saw everything that He had made, and behold, it was very good". But one thing was not good: that man should be alone. He needed a help answering to him. And it says, the LORD God caused a deep sleep to fall upon the man, and he slept; and He took one of his ribs and closed up the flesh instead thereof: and the rib, which the LORD God had taken from the man, made He a woman, and brought her unto the man.

That was the first marriage, beautiful in its simplicity, and God officiated at it. When Adam woke from his sleep, God presented him with his bride, beautiful, perfect from the hand of God. And Adam said, "This is now bone of my bones, and flesh of my flesh; she shall be called Woman, because she was taken out of Man." She belonged to him because she was part of him. She had been taken out of his side. She was literally a member of his body. And so are we who belong to the Lord Jesus. "We are members of His body" says the apostle in Ephesians chapter 5. "Christ also loved the Church, and gave Himself up for it." He passed through the deep sleep of death that He might have us to be with Him for ever. "This mystery is great" said the apostle, "but I speak in regard of Christ and of the Church."

It is indeed a great mystery. I am sure the full wonder of it will only be understood when we reach the glory. But this much we can grasp and enjoy right now, that we belong to Christ as surely as Eve belonged to Adam. We have been given to Him by His Father, joined to Him as members of His Body. And we shall be with Him for ever, "the fulness of Him that filleth all in all."

4) THE SON OF MAN

On the sixth day of creation God said "Let Us make man in Our image, after Our likeness: and let them have dominion over the fish ... the fowl the cattle, and over all the earth, and over every creeping thing". So Adam was given absolute control of all God's creation on earth. David refers to this in the 8th Psalm.

He had been considering the greatness of God's vast creation, and he exclaim "What is man, that Thou art mindful of him? and the son of man, that Thou visitest him? For Thou host made him but little lower than God, and crownest him with glory and honour. Thou modest him to have dominion over the works of Thy hands; Thou hast put all things under his feet ..."

Clearly David was thinking back to Adam's glory in the garden of Eden, but was that all? No, the Spirit of God was guiding him, perhaps into deeper thoughts than David himself realized at the time. For the epistle to the Hebrews says, concerning our Lord Jesus, "For not unto angels did He subject the world to come, whereof we speak". And then the write quotes some of these very words of David from Psalm 8. He makes it very clear that it is to the Lord Jesus he is referring, for he says, "We behold Him, who hath been made for a little while lower than the angels, even Jesus, because of the suffering of death crowned with glory and honour, that by the grace of God He should taste death for every man."

Most people when they read that verse think about our Lord Jesus crowned with glory and honour when He returned in resurrection to His place at God's right hand. And so He was. But in the context of this verse I believe it refers to the Lord Jesus in the glory and honour of perfect Manhood. When He took to Himself our humanity He occupied the place Adam had forfeited through sin. God set Him over the work of His hands and all things were subject to Him. When He was in the wilderness, you remember, being tempted of Satan, He was with the wild beasts but they did Him no harm, for they were under His control.

And in that glory and honour of perfect Manhood He one day took a heavy cross upon His back and went to Calvary and died for us. Had there been anything at all to mar His perfection, then His offering of Himself would never have atoned for sin. But there was not. In Him was no sin. And in that glory and honour of absolute perfection He tasted death for every one of us.

5) MAN OF SORROWS

There is an account in the third chapter of Genesis which does not refer primarily to the Lord Jesus, but we can hardly read it without thinking of Him. I refer to the curse which Adam brought upon himself because of his disobedience. God said, "Because thou host hearkened unto the voice of thy wife, and host eaten of the tree, of which I commanded thee, saying, Thou shalt not eat of it: cursed is the ground for thy sake; in toil shalt thou eat of it all the days of thy life; thorns also and thistles shall it bring forth to thee; and thou shalt eat the herb of the field; in the sweat of thy face shalt thou eat bread, till thou return unto the ground; for out of it wast thou taken: for dust thou art, and unto dust shalt thou return."

What a sad, sad tale. In the sweat of his brow he would toil to produce from the ground sufficient to eat, but along with the plants there would grow thorns and thistles to hinder his work, and in the end he would return to the dust from which his body had been taken. And so it was, exactly as God had said. But thankfully, not for all time. Oh no, for as soon as Adam fell God was right there with His promise of a Saviour. What wonderful love, loving His creatures still, despite their rebellion. And in the fulness of time God sent forth His Son, born of a woman. He took a body like ours, and in that human body He bore all the sorrows which have come upon man as a result of sin.

Yes, the sweat, the sorrows, the toil, the tears. He took His part in all of them. A man of sorrows He was, and well acquainted with grief. In Gethsemane's garden His soul was exceeding sorrowful even to death, and as He poured out His heart to God in heaven, the sweat came from His forehead like drops of blood. And then rough soldiers came and took Him to Pilate's hall and He allowed them to mock Him both clothing Him in a purple robe and taking a crown of twisted thorns they pressed it on His brow. Friends who have visited the holy land tell me these thorns still grow in the hedgerows, long flexible thorns which can easily be twisted into the shape of a crown. And Matthew tells us that when they had crowned Him and knelt before Him in mockery, they took the reed Out of His hand and smote Him on the head, doubtless driving the thorns deeper into His brow.

When men had done their worst, God dealt with Him in those lonely hours of darkness when He made His soul an offering for sin. And He said "Thou hast brought Me into the dust of death." But, "with His stripes we are healed"!

6) THE SIN OFFERING

The Lord Jesus told the Jews who did not believe on Him, "If ye believed Moses, ye would believe Me; for He wrote of Me". And in saying that He set His seal to the first five books of our Bible. They all tell us about Christ and I invite you to share with me another picture of our Lord Jesus in the third chapter of Genesis. You remember that when Adam and Eve sinned through disobedience they were immediately conscious of the change that had taken place. They knew they were naked and they were ashamed and to try and cover themselves they sewed fig leaves together and made themselves aprons. But that was a poor and inadequate covering. And the Bible record says "the LORD God made for Adam and for his wife coats of skins, and clothed them".

That is a word of pure grace. It shows how much God cared for them, despite their rebellion. In His love He took an animal - maybe more than one - and killing them, He took the skins and made garments to clothe them. Yes, He clothed them. God did it all Himself. What thoughts must have filled God's heart as the animals' lives were taken to meet the need of Adam and his wife. It's the first indication we have in our Bibles of the need for blood shedding, and one of the earliest illustrations of the Lord Jesus meeting that need at Calvary. "Apart from the shedding of blood there is no remission" is God's unfailing word.

Paul puts the whole truth into one precious verse at the end of the fifth chapter of 2nd Corinthians, "Him who knew no sin He made to be sin on our behalf; that we might become the righteousness of God in Him". Notice it was all done by God Himself. He provided the animal, shed its blood and then HE clothed the man and his wife. It was God's provision throughout. Adam had no part in it, except to received what God had done, teaching us the great lesson that salvation is of the Lord.

Many people are still sewing their fig leaves together, trying to provide their own covering, to work for their own righteousness. Basically all the religions of the world have this one thing in common. They teach there is good in men which must be encouraged and that by our own effort we must work for our salvation. But God says otherwise. Salvation is not of works, He says, that no man should glory. Right at the beginning of our Bibles He has shown us that He is the One who provides our salvation, and He has done it through the death of His Son at Calvary. There is no other way that our need can be met.

7) THE WOMAN'S SEED

When I was in Burma some years ago there was a fine Burmese man in the church who was a retired Inspector of Schools. He had a great love for his Bible. He began studying it when he was a graduate in Rangoon University, and one of his earliest recollections was being taught the first Messianic prophecy. That is the first promise of the Messiah who was to come. He often referred to it and taught us lessons from it. And I would like to share with you some of the lessons I learned from him. The verse is found in Genesis 3 in the portion where God spoke to the serpent and said "I will put enmity between thee and the woman, and between thy seed and her seed: it shall bruise thy head, and thou shalt bruise his heel". That is the very first direct reference to the Lord Jesus in our Bibles. He is spoken of as the woman's Seed.

That is a unique expression. In the birth of our Lord Jesus there was no man involved. He was born of a virgin, and God told Mary very plainly how it would happen. "The Holy Spirit shall come upon thee, and the power of the Most High shall overshadow thee: wherefore also that which is to be born shall be called Holy, the Son of God". Great is the mystery of Godliness; He who was manifested in the flesh. And we bow in worship as we ponder the wonderful way in which God's holy Son came into human experience.

And from the beginning the word of God has proved true, that there has been enmity between the Devil and the woman and between his seed and her seed. "It shall bruise thy head" God said "and thou shalt bruise his heel". And that happened, too. At Calvary the Lord Jesus was bruised for our iniquities. But that only for a little while - only His heel, as it were - for He rose again from the dead on the third day, triumphant over all His foes. And the Bible says, in Romans 16, "the God of peace shall bruise Satan under your feet shortly".

That day is coming. Satan still has a limited amount of power today, and we are told to be watchful, for our adversary the Devil, as a roaring lion, walks about, seeking whom he may devour. So let us be on our guard, and at the same time thank God that His very first promise about His Son will eventually find its complete fulfilment when the great Deceiver will be cast for ever into the lake of fire and brimstone.

8) THE IMAGE OF GOD

I was talking recently with a gentleman who believed that death ended all. "We die like the animals" he said, "and when we are gone that is the end of us". I drew his attention to the verses in Genesis chapter 1 where God said "Let us make man in our image, after our likeness" and the following verse says, "God created man in His own image, in the image of God created He him". That very fact makes us different from God's animal creation. We have been made in the likeness of God, with minds that can reason and communicate, and we have been made to enjoy fellowship with God. Sadly, that likeness was marred on account of sin, and later on, in Genesis chapter 5 it says about Adam that he lived a hundred and thirty years and became the father of a son in his own likeness, after his image, and named him Seth. The son still bore a resemblance to God, with a will to choose what was right, but the perfect image of God had been spoiled because of sin.

And that is where the coming of the Lord Jesus has made all the difference, for 2nd Corinthians chapter 5 says, "if any man is in Christ, he is a new creature". God began again in Christ, and Romans chapter 8 teaches us that every born again person is destined to be conformed to the image of His Son, in order that He might be the firstborn among many brethren. And the Son, of course, as we so well know, is the image of God. In fact, He is "the very image of His substance", or as another version puts it, "the very stamp of His nature" (Hebrews 1:3). As a coin or a seal pressed into molten wax makes an impression which is exactly the same as its own image, so the Lord Jesus is the very same as God His Father, in nature and in essence.

And we are going to be like Him. The image that was marred through sin has been restored through Christ and through eternal ages God is going to have many sons who will all bear the likeness of His only begotten Son. "Conformed to the image of His Son." And it will all happen in a moment of time, for when our Saviour returns He will change our lowly body to be like His glorious body. And how? we may ask. God gives us the answer, "by the power which enables Him even to subject all things to Himself" (Philippians 3:21 RSV).

9) THE LAST ADAM

When the Lord Jesus joined the two who were walking to Emmaus, it says "beginning from Moses and from all the prophets, He interpreted to them in all the Scriptures the things concerning Himself". We have been enjoying together some of the glimpses of Christ we find in the early chapters of Genesis. Adam is presented to us as the first man, and the apostle Paul comments on that fact in his first epistle to the Corinthians, when he says, "the first man Adam became a living soul. The last Adam became a life-giving Spirit."

So Adam heads up a race of men who receive life as he received it, from the great Creator. But alas, through his disobedience to God's plain word, he passed on to them the awful result of sin, which is death. In Romans 5 we read, "through one man sin entered into the world, and death through sin; and so death passed unto all men, for that all sinned." Adam is described as a figure of Christ, but he stands in contrast to Him. "The first man is of the earth, earthy: the second man is of heaven". Adam led men into sin and death, but the Lord Jesus came to suffer death on our behalf, and to lead many sons to glory.

I like the way the apostle Paul puts it in Romans 5:19, "through the one man's disobedience the many were made sinners, even so through the obedience of the One! How much is contained in those few words. He was always obedient, of course. He delighted to do His Father's will. But in Hebrews 5 we read that He "learned obedience by the things which he suffered", which I understand to mean that through life's experience of suffering He was constantly learning what obedience cost. He learned it in daily experience. And every suffering He endured resulted in glory to His God and Father in heaven.

Never did obedience cost a man more than it cost the Lord Jesus when He went out from Gethsemane's garden to give Himself upon the Cross. "Nevertheless not my will, but Thine be done" He said, and He went out to become obedient even unto death, yea, the death of the cross. Thank God through His obedience the many have been made righteous, just as many as will receive it by faith. And now He invites us to be obedient to Him, by obeying His commandments and following where He leads the way.

10) THE AMEN

I was visiting Niagara recently with a friend, and was impressed all over again by the sound of many waters as they hurled themselves over the Horseshoe Falls. And spanning the waters in the sky was the most beautiful rainbow, shining brightly in all its colours. I am told the rainbow can be seen any day between 2 and 4 p.m. when the sun is shining. I went back to my Bible to read about the first time God put His bow in the cloud. It was after the Flood, you remember, when Noah came out of the ark, that God made a covenant with all mankind that while the earth remains, seedtime and harvest, cold and heat, summer and winter, day and night, shall not cease. And then He said "I do set My bow in the cloud, and it shall be a token of the covenant between Me and the earth". It was something men could look at, and remember that God always keeps His promises.

But more than that - and I had not noticed this before - it was something for God to look at, too. "The bow shall be in the cloud; and I will look upon it" He said, "that I may remember the everlasting covenant". So that bow in the cloud which many thousands of tourists to Niagara gaze upon every year is seen also by God in heaven - a reminder to Him and to us that His word can never fail. He always keeps His promises.

When John the aged apostle got a glimpse into heaven he saw the throne of God, and he said there was a rainbow round about the throne like an emerald to look upon. Ezekiel saw it, too, hundreds of years before. And describing the brightness around God's throne he said, "as the appearance of the bow that is in the cloud in the day of rain, so was the appearance of the brightness round about". God's throne is a' rainbow-circled throne, a constant reminder that His word can never fail.

It tells us about Christ too, for in the first chapter of Paul's second letter to the Corinthians, he says, "the Son of God, Jesus Christ, who was preached among you ... was not yea and nay, but in Him is yea. For how many soever be the promises of God, in Him is the yea: wherefore also through Him is the Amen, unto the glory of God through us". Precious, is it not? all God's promises are made real to us in Christ, they reach us through Him. And through Christ we say Yes to them by faith.

So every time you see the rainbow in the sky, yes, and even when you do not, remember that Father, Son and Holy Spirit are all pledged to make sure to us the promises with which Scripture abounds. Oh how favoured we are!

11) GOD'S BELOVED SON

Genesis chapter 5 gives us the generations of Adam through to the days of Noah, and of each of the men mentioned, except one, it says "and he died". Those words run like a refrain through the whole chapter: "and he died". As though God would impress upon us for all time that the Devil is a liar from the beginning, for you remember he told Eve, "Ye shall not surely die". But he was wrong, as this chapter makes abundantly clear. One generation of men after another lived, begat sons and daughters, and then they died, with the exception of one man. It is recorded, "Enoch walked with God: and he was not; for God took him."

The 11th chapter of Hebrews has a fine commentary on that. It says, "By faith Enoch was translated that he should not see death; and he was not found, because God translated him: for before his translation he hath had witness borne to him that he had been well-pleasing unto God". We also make it our aim to be well-pleasing unto Him, wrote the apostle Paul to the Corinthians, but how? Surely in the same way as Enoch did - Enoch walked with God. What was involved in that, we may ask. Well, there must have been agreement for, "shall two walk together, except they have agreed?" asks Amos the prophet. Enoch must have agreed with God that he would walk where God led the way. And then step by step and day by day he kept to his promise and walked in fellowship with God. And God bore witness to him that he had been well-pleasing to Him.

It turns our thoughts to the One of whom the Father said, "This is My beloved Son, in whom I am well pleased". What a declaration that was from heaven! Peter speaks about it in his epistle; he says, "He received from God the Father honour and glory, when there came such a voice to Him from the excellent glory, 'This is My beloved Son, in whom I am well pleased'". He was surely the One to whom Micah the prophet referred when he said, "He hath shewed thee, O man, what is good; and what doth the Lord require of thee, but to do justly, and to love mercy, and to walk humbly with thy God?" He was God's perfect answer to what was required. He was the absolute expression of that which was good. No-one but God could answer to it completely and absolutely.

How lovely to contemplate the life on earth of God's beloved Son and then to remember that He has left us an example, that we should follow His steps. Let us increasingly seek God's help to do so, and then, maybe, some day God will bear witness to us that we also have been well-pleasing to Him.

12) THE LAMB OF GOD

In the third chapter of Genesis some of the awful consequences of sin are presented to us. For instance, the way to the garden of Eden was closed to Adam and his wife, guarded by the cherubim with flaming sword. But while the book of Genesis presents the beginnings of human experience, the book of Revelation presents the end of it, at least the end of what is recorded, and it is interesting and thrilling to compare the third chapter of Genesis with the final two chapters of Revelation. For instance, the gates of the eternal city are for ever open. And the way to the tree of life which was barred when Adam sinned is now open to all who have washed their robes, for they have the right to come to the tree of life and to enter in by the gates to the city.

In Genesis 3 the curse is imposed. But in Revelation chapter 22 verse 3 it says, "there shall be no curse any more". Then again, sorrow and death came in through sin, but both are abolished when you come to Revelation 21. "Death shall be no more" God says, and "He shall wipe away every tear from their eyes", and moreover there will be no mourning, nor crying, nor pain any more, for these are the first things, and they are passed away for ever.

God's fellowship with His creatures was interrupted on account of sin. No longer could He come to talk with Adam in the garden. And there is no doubt that God felt that loss more keenly than ever Adam did. But when you turn to Revelation 21, all that God lost is restored, for the tabernacle of God is with men, and "they shall be His peoples, and God Himself shall be with them, and be their God".

But why so great a change? Between the books of Genesis and the Revelation comes the story of the Saviour's life and death and of His glorious resurrection. He is the Lamb of God foretold in Genesis, and He bore the sin of the world when He gave Himself in death at Calvary. And in the Revelation He is seen in all His glory as the Lamb standing in the midst of the throne. The throne of God and of the Lamb is the very centre of the eternal city and out of it proceeds the river of water of life, bright as crystal. So while death came in as a result of sin in the book of Genesis and produced its awful trail throughout the Bible record, by the close of God's revelation we see sin and death conquered for ever and the Lord Jesus is triumphant over all.

III

THE TABERNACLE IN ONE HOUR

14

INTRODUCTION

The Tabernacle which was built by the people of Israel under Moses' leadership in the Sinai desert, was God's dwelling-place where He lived among His people. They lived in their tents round about and God's tent was in the centre. So they actually had the eternal God living in their midst. It was God's idea, for He said: "Let them make Me a sanctuary; that I may dwell among them" (Exodus chapter 25:8). He gave them in detail the pattern to which it had to be built, and when it was completed He showed His approval by filling it with His presence. So the children of Israel had the double privilege of having Jehovah, the living God, dwelling in their midst. This distinguished them from all the other nations of the world. Moses made this point when he said, "What other nation is so great as to have their gods near them the way the LORD our God is near us whenever we pray to Him?"

The answer is, "No nation!" Theirs was a unique privilege and we begin by asking why? Moses comes to our help again and he gives us part of the answer in Deuteronomy chapter 7:7 where he says, "The LORD did not set His affection on you and choose you because you were more numerous than other peoples, for you were the fewest of all peoples. But it was because the LORD loved you and kept the oath He sware to your fore fathers that He brought you out with a mighty hand and redeemed you from the land of slavery, from the power of Pharaoh king of Egypt."

It was partly because of their forefathers, Abraham and Isaac and Jacob. Abraham was God's friend who at the call of God, left his home and country, and God brought him into the land of Canaan which He promised to give to him and his descendants. And from his grandson Jacob, whose name God changed to Israel, He provided the leaders of the twelve tribes which made up this new nation. God took Israel's family into Egypt at a time of world-wide famine, and there they served the Egyptians. But God hadn't forgotten them, nor the promises He made to their fathers, and He sent Moses to deliver them from their bondage; and the story of how He did so is full of instruction for us.

Let me remind you briefly of the Passover night when the destroying angel passed through the land of Egypt, and according to God's Word the firstborn in each Israeli family was sheltered from death by the blood of the lamb sprinkled on the doorposts and lintel of his home. God said, "When I see the blood I will pass over you," and it has all got a present-day lesson for us, for in 1 Corinthians chapter 5 we are reminded that Christ our Passover has been sacrificed for us. God had plainly said that apart from the shedding of blood there is no forgiveness of sin, and that is why our Lord Jesus went to Calvary and died, so that His blood might cleanse us from all our sin.

Which makes me want to pause for a moment to ask if you are sheltered by the blood? Or to put it another way, have you believed in the Lord Jesus, that He is God's Son and that He died for you? That is where we begin in our experience with God. The night Israel was redeemed from Egypt God changed their calendar and made it the first month of their year. He gave them a new start. And so He does for us, when we come to Christ, for the Bible says, "if anyone is in Christ he is a new creation; the old has gone, the new has come."

Then God led them out of Egypt and through the Red Sea where they were baptized unto Moses in the cloud and. in the sea. He was their new leader and at Sinai God called him up into the mountain where He gave him His law to pass on to His people. When they pledged their willingness to obey, Moses sprinkled with blood both the people and the book in which God's law was written and so they became the people of the book; and then, notice, it was only THEN God asked them to build Him a house that He might dwell amongst them.

That is an important point which I would stress to our hearts at the beginning of our study. The people who built a house for God were first of all redeemed by blood, baptised in water and then constituted a nation on their pledged obedience to His Word It is extremely important, for what we learn from Israel's experience its New Testament counterpart. God has a house today, but it is a spiritual house built of living stones, as 1 Peter chapter 2 teaches us. These living ones as they are called, are disciples of the Lord Jesus redeemed by His precious blood as Peter explains, baptized by immersion in water in acknowledgement of Christ's claims upon them and then built together in obedience to His Word.

And if you turn to the opening words of Peter's epistle you will notice he addresses those to whom he is writing as "elect according to the foreknowledge of God the Father, in sanctification of the Spirit, unto obedience and sprinkling of the blood of Jesus Christ," and you will agree Peter must surely have had in mind the time when the people in the new nation of Israel were sprinkled by blood.

The parallel between their experience and ours is very plain to see and as we pursue our study of this exciting subject we should be continually looking from the shadows of the Old Testament to the substance of the New, and asking ourselves, what lesson does God want me to learn from that? It is an exciting subject, for if God has a house on earth today then we want a part in it, don't we?

15

THE PATTERN

When God was about to bring the children of Israel out of Egypt after their long years of bondage He sent a message through Moses to the Pharaoh, "Let My people go that they may serve Me." Pharaoh hesitated a long time before he finally obeyed, as a result of which his nation suffered the awful plagues. But God never changed His message. "Let My people go that they may serve Me."

There is a sense in which that message was to His people as well as to Egypt's king, and they may well have asked, where does God want us to serve Him? And how? The Tabernacle He asked them to build was His answer to these questions. It was a house for God to dwell in, so that His long-felt desire might be realised at last, to have a dwelling-place in the very centre of His people's lives. What a wonder that the living God who inhabits eternity, who dwells in the high and holy place, should desire also to dwell among men on earth. But so it is. Years later king Solomon pondered the wonder of it when he said "Will God really dwell on earth? The heavens, even the highest heaven, cannot contain You. How much less this temple I have built." It is wonderful and the more I think about it, the more wonderful it seems. That is why I am so glad you are studying this subject, for I do believe it is one which is very near to the heart of God.

Notice that His house was not only a place for God to dwell but also the place where they served Him. To the house of God they brought all their gifts and their sacrifices for sin. And the books of Moses are full of detailed instruction about how God wanted to be serve? There is both a place to serve and a way to serve, and God intends His instructions to Israel to furnish us with lessons about our worship and service today.

When they came into the land and the Tabernacle was set up in one settled place rather than. moving from place to place, God insisted they must come to this one place only. "You shall not offer your gifts in every place," He said, "but in the place which the LORD your God shall choose, to put His Name there." That is an important point which is emphasized many times in Deuteronomy chapter 12. Now let us return to Exodus chapter 25 for a more careful look at God's instructions about His house. We noticed that when Moses had read all God's commandments to the people and they had pledged themselves to obey, they were constituted a holy nation and a kingdom of priests. Then God said to Moses, in Exodus chapter 25:2, "Speak to the children of Israel, that they take for Me an offering; of every one whose heart makes him willing you shall take My offering." And then verses 8 and 9: "And let them make Me a sanctuary that I may dwell among them. According to all that I show you, the pattern of the tabernacle and the pattern of all the furniture, even so shall you make it."

So the willing-hearted ones brought their gifts and the wise-hearted, men and women, worked each in their sphere, to build those materials into a house for God, according to the pattern He had given them. That they build to the pattern was of primary importance, for God repeated it a few times, and the point is made again in Hebrews chapter 8. And the reason given is most interesting. Verse 5 says "they serve at a sanctuary which is a copy and a shadow of what is in heaven." This is why Moses was warned when he was about to build the Tabernacle, "See to it that you make everything according to the pattern shown you on the mountain." So Moses was shown the original in heaven and then sent down to build a copy of it on earth. No wonder God was so insistent it should be built to His pattern, and that the pattern was so full of detail. And the lesson for us is equally clear. God's house today is a spiritual house as opposed to the material buildings of Old Testament days, but He is just as interested in it, perhaps even more so.

And there is a pattern to be followed as the apostle Paul reminds us. His final letter before he died was written to Timothy and he said, "Hold the pattern of sound words which you heard from me, in faith and love which is in Christ Jesus." That strong appeal comes down to our hearts today, and we cannot escape it for we are called to build God's house just as Timothy was. And there is a pattern for collective worship and service laid out in the New Testament, which we are instructed to follow and also to pass on to others. Remembering the importance God placed on this we might well ask ourselves, am I building for God according to the pattern of His Word?

One more instructive point which comes out of our reading; God's house was built out of the materials they brought as a freewill offering. Gold is the first thing mentioned in the long list God gave them, and it set me thinking; those who gave their gold for the making of the golden calf may have had none left when this opportunity came for the building of God's house. If so, what a disappointment that must have been. But there were plenty who were able to give and they did so generously, for a few chapters further on we read about Moses restraining them, because there was more than enough. Great days they were! And when God's spiritual house was in building in the days of the apostles it says about the Macedonian disciples, "their deep poverty abounded unto the riches of their liberality" (2 Corinthians 8:3).

They pleaded to be allowed to give and Paul put his finger on the secret when he wrote, "first they gave their own selves to the Lord." Lovely, wasn't it? They themselves were built as living stones on the foundation of the teaching of Christ and His apostles which Paul and others had laid, for Paul was a wise master-builder and then they built on that same foundation themselves. Built on to it by their teaching and service such as the apostle likened to gold, silver and precious stones which will come through the fiery testing of that great accounting day and be found to the praise and glory of the Master that they served. Which prompts me to raise the question: Where are you and I building today, and what are we laying up for eternity on that firm foundation for God?

16

THE COURT AND THE GATE

The Tabernacle in the wilderness was so called because in the wilderness of Sinai God gave instructions for it and that is where it was built. It was a portable building and the people of Israel carried it with them as they journeyed through the desert. When the pillar of cloud moved the people packed up and the priests and Levites made themselves busy packing the Tabernacle and transporting it to their next stopping place, wherever the pillar of cloud halted. The God who lived amongst them was their Guide throughout their forty years of journeying. We now come to consider the white linen curtains which formed the court of the Tabernacle, for in our study we are working from the outside in.

The twelve tribes of Israel lived in orderly arrangement around God's house, three tribes on each side and if you came out of any of the tents on the North, South or West sides you would be confronted with a wall of white linen. It was about nine feet high, higher than any person could see over, and according to Revelation chapter 19 white linen speaks about righteousness and in this case the righteousness of God. "Thy righteousness, O God, is very high" the psalmist said, and as we can see, it shut men out from the presence of God. It was a constant reminder of the fact that all have sinned and fallen short of the glory of God. It was upheld by pillars secured in the desert sand by sockets of brass, telling us of God's judgement, and we recall another psalmist said, "Righteousness and judgement are the foundation of Thy throne."

But if you read God's careful instructions in Exodus chapter 27, you will see there were silver hooks which held the curtains up and the pillars were joined by silver bands and the silver was obtained from the atonement money. So although the tall white curtains seemed to be barring the way to God, there was a message of redemption too. There was a way into God and anyone who followed those white curtains around would come eventually to the East side, where there was a beautiful gate of blue, purple, scarlet and fine linen. It was a wide gate, about thirty-six feet across, room for all to come, and of course it speaks to us about Christ, the only Way to God.

It was nine feet high and a verse in Exodus chapter 38 says, "it was answerable to the hangings of the court" - a precious word, reminding us the Lord Jesus did not fall short of God's standards. He answered to them. The only Man who ever lived on earth who measured up completely to the righteousness of God; he came to share that righteousness with us, and we remind ourselves that when a person entered through the gate he was completely hidden. They enveloped him, as it were, reminding us of Paul's testimony in Philippians chapter 3, that he desired to "gain Christ and be found in Him, not having a righteousness of my own that comes from the law, but which is through faith in Christ – the righteousness that comes from God and is by faith."

Thank God for the glorious gospel message, for in it a righteousness from God is revealed, a righteousness which is by faith from first to last. That is, the lesson of the white linen curtains of the court.

Now think with me about the gate of embroidered work which was constantly inviting people to come. It was on the East side, you remember, and when Cain went out from the presence of the Lord he went toward the East. So anyone coming to God would have his back to the East and he would be confronted with this beautiful gate of blue, purple, scarlet and fine linen. Blue is the heavenly colour, telling of the One who said, "I am from heaven above," the Son of God from heaven. And He was born a King as purple reminds us. The cochus worm provided the dye for the scarlet and tells of the lowliness of Christ, a Man amongst men. "Behold the Man" said Pontius Pilate and he spoke better than he knew that day, for there was never a Man to compare with Him. He was God's Man, a Leader of a new creation.

And the fine linen we have already stated speaks of righteousness, and tells of God's righteous Servant. The gate was upheld by four pillars and we must surely think of the four gospel-writers who have lifted up the Person and the work of Christ to the gaze of the world. How we thank God for the fourfold presentation of Christ, Matthew presenting Him as King and tracing His ancestry back to David, Israel's great king, and still further back to Abraham the father of the Jewish nation. Mark presents Him as the Servant and so without genealogy he plunges into his story of God's Servant at work in the prime of His manhood. Luke presents Him in the scarlet colour as the Son of Man and characteristically His genealogy goes back to the beginning of time and shows Him to be the son of Adam, the Son of God.

But John reminds us that He is the timeless One, without beginning of days for, "In the beginning was the Word, and the Word was with God and the Word was God.The same was in the beginning with God." Majestic words! What a wonderful person He is, very God and yet very Man, born a King yet dying on the cross, and all so that He could become our Saviour and open up a way into God's presence for those who had fallen far away through sin. Thank God that the One who has opened a way to God for all who are willing to come is Jehovah Tsidkenu, the Lord is our righteousness.

17

THE BRAZEN ALTAR OF BURNT OFFERING

The Tabernacle built under Moses' leadership in the Sinai desert was God's dwelling place on earth. The Epistle to the Hebrews tells us it is a parable for our time, so obviously God intends us to learn lessons from it about the way we should worship and serve Him today. That is why it is so important a study. Indeed I suggest to you that it is difficult to understand the epistle to the Hebrews without a knowledge of the Tabernacle, for its teaching is based on what happened in the tabernacle service.

Entering the courtyard by the beautiful gate, which was the subject of our last chapter, the worshipper was confronted by the brazen altar, the altar of burnt offering, as it was called, and we must now consider its teaching. It dominated the courtyard for it was nine feet square and about five feet high. This was where the sacrifices were offered and it speaks to us about Christ in death. If the gate speaks of Christ in His life, the altar is Christ in His death.

It was a busy altar, at least when Israel was right with God it was. You might say it served as a barometer of their spiritual condition, for if the

79

altar was neglected it was an indication the hearts of the people were out of touch with God. To this altar they brought their burnt offerings and their peace offerings. They were both worship offerings, the means God provided for them to express their appreciation and love for Him. And to it also they brought their sin offerings. These animals were killed at the altar but burned outside the camp. Only the fat and inwards of sin offerings were burned on the brazen altar. The worship offerings were voluntary. They might or might not be offered according to a person's or a family's own wish, but the sin offerings were compulsory if a person was to walk in fellowship with God.

So lots of animals' blood was shed at this altar and the priests and Levites were kept very busy, and it all pointed forward to the one great Sacrifice on Calvary when Christ offered Himself without blemish unto God and at the same time bore our sins in His body upon the tree. One sacrifice for sins for ever" is the way the writer to the Hebrews sums it up, and another verse in that same tenth chapter says we have been sanctified through the offering of the body of Jesus Christ once for all." Glorious words! Once for all and for ever. Christ's work at Calvary was complete and final and all the sacrifices offered at this altar in God's house pointed forward to it.

The altar of burnt offering was made of acacia wood, which in one translation of the Old Testament is called incorruptible wood because of its endurance, and that is appropriate for it tells of the humanity of our Lord Jesus, who was originally "in the form of God, but counted it not a thing to be grasped to be on equality with God, but emptied Himself, taking the form of a Servant, being made in the likeness of men; and being found in fashion as a Man, He humbled Himself, becoming obedient unto death, yea, the death of the Cross."

He took our manhood in order that He might go to the Cross and die for us, and for that He was specially strengthened, as we are reminded by the fact that the wood was overlaid with brass, though most probably it was copper. The altar was made to stand the fire which consumed the sacrifices; and it was not ordinary fire. That would never have been able to consume all the animal flesh which came to this altar; it was the fire of God which came down from heaven. Reminding us that when the Saviour died it was not just the cruelty of men He suffered, bitter as that was, or even the fierce attacks of Satan and his hosts of evil, but the Isaiah scripture says, "the LORD laid on Him the iniquity of us all." In those three lonely hours of darkness He was bearing our sin in His body on the tree, and I believe He was specially strengthened by God for the experience. In Psalm 80, Asaph seems to touch on it when he says, "Let Thy hand be upon the Man of Thy right band, upon the Son of Man whom Thou madest strong for Thyself."

The fire never went out on the altar, so that whatever time of the day or night you might pass by the gate you would see the tire burning. The priests placed wood on it in the morning and on top of the wood the morning sacrifice, a young lamb as a burnt offering. And in the evening another lamb was offered. It was a continuing offering morning and evening of every day, and it is precious to remember that the little lamb in the morning would have died about the same time as the Saviour was nailed and crucified and the lamb in the evening died at the same time as He bowed His head and gave up His spirit.

There is little doubt that is what God had in mind when He gave instructions for this to happen. And we are left to ponder what this must have meant to God as He smelled the sweet fragrance of these offerings morning by morning and evening by evening. It all spoke so poignantly of the coming sacrifice of His Son. And I ask, what does it mean to you and me as we look back upon it? Happy we are if we can say, and sing,

> "I have been to the altar
> And witnessed the Lamb,
> Burnt wholly to ashes for me;
> And watched its sweet savour
> Ascending on high,
> Accepted, O God, by Thee."

18

THE LAVER

The Tabernacle or Sanctuary in the wilderness was the place where the people of Israel served God according to His careful instructions and they were represented before God by the priests whom God appointed for them from the sons of Aaron. We now consider the laver which stood between the brazen altar and the entrance to the holy place. This was where the priests would begin their day. God's instruction was very clear in Exodus chapter 30; before they started their service either in the tent of meeting or at the altar of burnt offering, they were to wash their hands and feet at the laver: the scripture says, "that they die not." That shows how seriously God viewed their service. It was holy service, for God was a holy God, and they must not come to it with unclean hands or feet.

It is interesting that the serving women provided the laver, for it was made out of their mirrors which they gave for the service of God. And that immediately gives us a clue as to what the laver speaks about, for James in his epistle refers to God's Word as a mirror in which we see ourselves. But the laver was also the place where defilement was washed away, and that is the wonderful thing about God's Word. It not only shows us our defilement, it has the power also to make us clean. "How can a young man keep his way pure?" asked the psalmist, and the answer was "By living according to Your Word."

There were two uses for the laver, and this is important for us to notice. Besides the day by day washing of hands and feet there was also an initial washing, we might call it bathing, for the whole of their body was washed when they were consecrated to their priestly office. This was done by Moses. They did not do it themselves. Before they were clothed in their priestly garments and anointed they were washed all over. This tells us of the work of our Lord Jesus, who has cleansed us by the washing of water with the Word. Ephesians chapter 5, and Titus chapter 3 speak about the same thing when it says, "according to His mercy He saved us through the washing of regeneration" and that is the word LAVER.

It is interesting how the New Testament scriptures carry us back to the Old Testament, and the one explains the other. This subject of the washing at the laver takes us in thought to the upper room where the Lord Jesus met His apostles on the evening before He died, and you remember how He washed their feet. Peter objected at first. "You shall never wash my feet," he said, until the Master pointed out the absolute necessity for it, and the conversation between them brings out some very important lessons for us. The Lord Jesus said, "he that is bathed only needs to wash his feet." So you get the point, there is the initial bathing when each believing one is washed clean by the application of God's Word to his heart.

The Lord Jesus spoke to Nicodemus about being born of water and the Spirit, and the water there is the water of God's Word which the Holy Spirit uses, to bring us to the experience of the new birth. After that, we need the daily washing to keep ourselves from defilement and it highlights to our hearts the absolute importance of our daily reading of

God's Word. It has a cleansing effect on our hearts. That is just one of its effects, of course. There are many others, for it feeds our souls, and gives light on our pathway, and teaches us what God wants us to know. And it is full of His great and precious promises which faith lays hold of, and by which we grow up into Christ. So let us not neglect the reading of our Bible, fellow Christian, for it is our very life. "The words I speak to you are spirit and are life," the Lord Jesus said.

So summing up we learn that the initial bathing is something the Lord Jesus Christ has done when He made us clean by the washing of the water of the Word, and that with the glorious prospect in view of our priestly service in God's house. We shall be thinking more about that later on, but let me just remind you of that important verse in 1 Peter chapter 2:5, "You also, as living stones, are built up a spiritual house, to be a holy priesthood, to offer up spiritual sacrifices, acceptable to God through Jesus Christ." We are passing through a world full of defilement and so we need the daily cleansing of the Word of God. Our hands, indicating what we do, and our feet, how we walk, must be cleansed by the effect of God's holy Word. And we can help one another in this, for you remember He said "If I then, the Lord and Master, have washed your feet, you also ought to wash one another's feet. For I have given you an example, that you also should do as I have done to you."

That is a heart-searching word indeed. By lowly acts of service done out of the love of Christ we can help one another to keep ourselves clean for God's holy service. "Having therefore these promises, beloved, let us cleanse ourselves from all defilement of flesh and spirit, perfecting holiness in the fear of God" (2 Corinthians 7:1).

19

THE CURTAINS AND THE COVERINGS

The subject of the Tabernacle is a fascinating one. God speaks about it as a parable for the present time so it is obvious He intends us to learn our lessons from all its detail about our service for Him, today. The Hebrew word MISHKAN, meaning 'dwelling place', is used in many places to describe the whole structure, the entire Tabernacle. But it also has a specialized application to the curtains which formed the inner covering over the golden boards.

There were two sets of curtains, the first made of fine linen, blue, purple and scarlet with figures of cherubim worked on them, and over that was a curtain of goats' hair. The beautiful curtains were called the tabernacle, which means dwelling place; and the goats' hair curtains were called the tent, meaning meeting place. So the tent covered the tabernacle, from which we learn the place where God dwells among His people on earth, is also the place where they meet with God. A very important point, and the more you think about it the more you realise the preciousness of the truth it contains. God said about this place, "there I will meet with you," and there is nothing more precious in life's experience than to meet with God in His dwelling place.

Let us think about the tabernacle curtains that were made of fine linen, blue, purple and scarlet. The materials were gifted by willing-hearted people, and wise-hearted women worked in their tents, spinning the yarn from which the curtains were made. So men and women worked together in the building of God's house, but each in their own sphere. There were ten curtains and they were all of the same size and design. Five of them were coupled together and then the other five; and the two fives were joined together by loops of blue and clasps of gold and the Bible record says, "the tabernacle shall be one" (Exodus 26:6). That is a significant statement, remembering as we do what a great value God places on unity among His people.

It is very obvious He gave instructions for the tabernacle to be made in this way because He wanted to teach to us an important lesson. God's house today is a spiritual house as we learn from 1 Peter chapter 2:5 and it is composed of individual churches of God which are joined together. Some speak of local churches as being autonomous but that is not how they were in New Testament days. They were very much linked together in groups or provinces, and then you will find as you study the Acts of the apostles and their letters, that the provinces were joined together to form a fellowship of churches which is called in 1 Corinthians chapter 1:9, "the Fellowship of God's Son, Jesus Christ our Lord." So it was a Fellowship which belonged to Him over which He was Lord and in which His Word was supreme.

The importance of this cannot be over-emphasized, for you will remember the Lord Jesus prayed very specially, just before He died, for those who would believe through the word of the apostles, "that they might all be one, that the world may believe that Thou didst send Me." And again He said, "that they may be perfected into one, that the world may know." That is in John chapter 17. He so much wanted His disciples to be together in a visible unity which the world could see and that is exactly what happened in the early days of the apostles' work. They went from place to place preaching the Word. Souls were saved and the saved ones were taught all the things the Lord Jesus commanded. Those who were obedient were then baptized in water and added together in churches of God and those churches were all built to the same pattern. The same teaching was given in each one, "as I teach everywhere in every church," Paul writes in 1 Corinthians 4:17; and the result was that they practised the same thing.

Paul and his fellow-workers were at pains to ensure the churches were linked together, and this was largely achieved by their having overseers (elders) in each church who were linked in a united elderhood. That the elderhood was united is clear from many scriptures. You will remember that at a time of famine the Church of God in Antioch sent a money gift to the churches in Judaea, and it says they sent it to the elders by the hand of Barnabas and Saul. There would be many churches of God in Judaea at that time, and how could that gift have been distributed if the elders had not been working together? You will remember also how Peter wrote his epistle to disciples in five provinces. There must have been many churches of God in those five provinces but one letter, served them all; for they were joined together, and so were the elders who cared for them, for in chapter 5 he addresses them together as one elderhood.

There are many such examples of the linking together of the churches of God in those New Testament days. I do believe it is a subject near to the heart of God. As the tabernacle was one, so God's house today must be one; all believing, teaching and practising the same truths presented to us in the Scriptures.

The tent of goats' hair was made in the same way, although in this case there were eleven curtains and they were a little longer than the curtains of the tabernacle so they completely covered them. And over the tent of goats' hair there was a covering first of rams' skins dyed red and a final outer covering of badger skins or sealskins. You may remember the ram that was used at the consecration of the priests and how its blood was applied to their ears, thumbs and great toes. It signified that they were all for God, giving themselves to this special service He had called them to. It reminds us also that if these truths of God's house are to be expressed today it will require men and women of similar dedication prepared to give themselves wholly to the Lord in obedience to His Word.

The outer covering of badger skins or seal skins was doubtless designed to give full protection from the elements. It certainly was not anything beautiful to look at. If you wanted to see the beauty of God's house you had to go inside. An interesting point, for it is largely so today. The beauty of God's house with its priestly service to God in worship and reaching out to men with His Word, is something which is appreciated mostly by those who engage in it. But more of that later when we go inside the holy place and learn our lessons from what the priests did day by day and week by week as they served God according to his instructions in that holy place.

20

THE BOARDS

We come now to the subject of the boards which formed the main structure of the building and which supported the tabernacle curtains. Exodus chapter 26:15 says, ''thou shalt make the boards for the tabernacle of acacia wood, standing up.'' Once they were growing as trees in the forest but they were felled and shaped and made ready for their place in God's house, as the Lord's disciples are when they are created anew in Christ Jesus and then by obedience to His Word made ready to stand with others in the service and testimony of a church of God. For not only does God want us to stand up for Him when we receive new life, "and having done all, to stand," says Ephesians 6:13; God also wants us to stand together for the truths He has laid out in His Word.

It is most instructive that when it says in Acts chapter 2 that those who received the word Peter preached on the day of Pentecost were baptized and there. were added unto them in that day; the word "added" means placed side by side. And that is what actually happened; they stood side by side to uphold the precious truths connected with God's dwelling place on earth. We noticed when we were studying the brazen altar that the acacia wood, or incorruptible wood as one translation puts it, spoke of the incorruptible humanity of Christ; and that interpretation still holds good, for when we are born again we become partakers of His nature. Our new nature is like His and cannot sin. Our old nature can, of course, and that is why we experience the struggle we do, our old self leading us into sin, and the Holy Spirit working through our new nature to lead us into a life well-pleasing to the Lord.

And the wooden boards were covered with gold, reminding us we are partakers in the divine nature. So Paul wrote about two of his brethren and said, if any enquire about them, "they are the messengers of the churches, they are the glory of Christ" (2 Corinthians 8:23). What a beautiful thought, that you and I can shine like gold in God's house, for His glory; for the precious sons of Zion are still comparable to fine gold as they were in Jeremiah's day (see Lamentations 4:2). Let us keep the gold shining bright as we live daily in touch with the Lord.

Each of these boards had two tenons (a type of joint which connects two pieces together) at the base which fitted into two sockets of silver - and these formed a solid foundation for the structure when it was erected on the desert sands. A very solid foundation and a very costly one too, for each socket was made of a talent of silver (a talent is an ancient measurement that, according to the experts, would have weighed between 25 and 50 kilograms). It opens up a most interesting study, for if you turn to Exodus chapter 30 you will read where the silver came from. It was from the atonement money. When a young Israelite reached the age of 20 he was numbered among God's people and at that time he paid half a shekel (weighing approximately 7 grams) into the nation's coffers. It was the same amount for everyone. The rich did not pay more, nor the poor less, and God said it was to be given as a ransom for their soul. Maybe you remember king David numbered his people once and evidently he did not collect this ransom money and a plague broke out among them.

It reminds us that the work of Christ in redemption is in three parts. We are redeemed from going down to the pit when we first put our trust in the Saviour, redeemed by His precious blood and that is something which can never be reversed. And when He comes again our bodies are going to be redeemed and that will complete His redemptive work. And in between there is another aspect of redemption which Titus chapter 2:14 speaks of: "Who gave Himself for us," one of the purposes for which Christ died, which sometimes we are apt to forget; "that He might redeem us from all iniquity" (lawlessness is perhaps a better translation), "and purify unto Himself a people for His own possession, zealous of good works." This passage of Scripture demands our careful thought, for it shows that Christ came to redeem us from all lawlessness, so that we no longer please ourselves, but acknowledging His Lordship we bow to His word.

When we do so we make a public expression of our decision by being baptized in water, after which we take our place in a church of God and are numbered among God's people. I say again this aspect of our redemption we do well to ponder carefully, for if we are going to find our place in the service of God's house we will need to make sure we are building on the firm foundation of His Word. The foundation is Christ, Paul wrote to the Corinthians (1 Corinthians 3:11), and in Ephesians chapter 2 he refers to "the foundation of the apostles and prophets."

But there is no contradiction, for the foundation the apostles built on was the teaching of Christ, and it has not changed from that day to this. The firm foundation of God still stands and God is still looking for obedient ones who will acknowledge that Christ is Lord and who will stand together to uphold the great truths of His dwelling place on earth. That is what the gold-covered boards did, standing in their silver sockets. God help us to learn the lessons they teach us and to take our place standing with others for the great truths of His house on earth today.

21

THE GOLDEN ALTAR OF INCENSE

As we continue our study of the Tabernacle, we remind ourselves that it was only the priests who served in the holy place. And behind the holy place, behind the veil, was the holy of holies, where God's presence was, and the high priest alone was allowed to go in, only once in the year, on the great day of atonement. It says in Hebrews chapter 9 that the priests go in continually into the first tabernacle, that is the holy place, "accomplishing the services". And it is this continual priestly service that we are considering together. We must always remember that the Tabernacle is a parable for the present time, and there is priestly service for us today. That is why the subject is so important and also why 1 Peter 2:5 is such a key verse: "You also, as living stones, are built up a spiritual house, to be a holy priesthood, to offer up spiritual sacrifices, acceptable to God through Jesus Christ.

Entering through the screen into the holy place, the priest would see immediately in front of him the golden altar where incense was burnt and from which a sweet fragrance ascended to God. It was made of acacia wood which we have suggested speaks of the incorruptible humanity of the Lord Jesus, and it was covered with pure gold, speaking of His glory and deity. So clearly it presents to us Christ in glory. I remember a fellow Christian telling me of a precious experience he once had. His daughter was rushed to hospital for an emergency operation and he was pacing the corridors of the hospital in such anxiety. But as he began to pray the thought struck him, 'there is a Man in the glory and He is there for me' and it was a tremendous comfort to his heart. This golden altar of incense teaches us that truth – there IS a Man in the glory, for the Lord Jesus has taken our humanity back to His Father's throne and there He lives forever to make intercession for us.

Every morning and evening it was the priest's responsibility to burn incense on this altar. The incense was made of four spices and was something specially for God. The people were not to make it or use it for themselves, for it spoke to God of the fragrance of the life and work of His dear Son. Continually the incense was burning in the holy place before the veil and therefore immediately in front of the mercy seat where God dwelt. It spoke to God's heart of the preciousness of His Son and David grasped something of its significance, for he said in Psalm 141, "Let my prayer be set forth as incense before Thee, the lifting up of my hands as the evening sacrifice." And you will remember that when the angel appeared to Zacharias with the surprising news he and his wife were to have a son in their old age, he was serving at the golden altar burning the incense and the people were praying outside.

Luke chapter 1 tells us about that. So clearly they understood their prayers ascended to God in the fragrance of that burning incense. What a precious lesson it brings to our hearts, for, "Thy Name is as ointment poured forth," the Song of Songs says, and the Lord Jesus invited us to present our prayers in His Name. It was not just a question of adding His Name to the end of our prayers. It has a far deeper meaning than that. The evening before He died when He was going over such important teaching with His apostles, He said, "Hitherto you have asked nothing in My Name; ask, and you shall receive, that your joy may be full." So that is the lesson which comes so preciously from the golden altar where the incense burned, that we have "a great High Priest. who has passed through the heavens, Jesus, the Son of God" [that is His High Priestly title]. "Let us therefore draw near with boldness to the throne of grace, that we may receive mercy, and may find grace to help us in time of need" (Hebrews 4:14,16).

Another important point to notice is that the fire by which the incense was burned was taken from the altar of burnt offering where the sacrifices were offered. Two of Aaron's sons made the fearful mistake of offering it with strange fire and they died before the Lord (Leviticus 10:1,7). It was so important, for Christ's death is the basis of all our communion with God. If there had been no fire at the copper altar there could have been no incense burning at the golden altar. Christ's work for us on His Father's throne is forever dependent upon His death at Calvary.

Let us heed the invitation to draw near through Him, for He ever lives to make intercession for us. We remember the Tabernacle was a copy and shadow of heavenly things, so we are not surprised to read in Revelation chapter 5 that the twenty-four elders before God's throne held golden bowls full of incense, which John said are the prayers of the saints. Revelation chapter 8 is even more explicit, for it says "another angel came and stood over the altar, having a golden censer; and there was given unto him much incense, that he should add it unto the prayers of the saints upon the golden altar which was before the throne. And the smoke of the incense, with the prayers of the saints, went up before God out of the angel's hand." What a glorious thought that is! It lifts the prayer meeting of the church to a very high plane when we remember our prayers go into these golden bowls which are before God's throne, and they are accepted before God in all the fragrance and worthiness of the One who is great priest over God's house. So set a great value upon the church prayer meeting, please, remembering that as in tabernacle days, so also today, it is part of the continual service of the priesthood. In the church of God in Jerusalem, the disciples continued steadfastly in the prayers, and we cannot do better than follow their example.

22

THE GOLDEN TABLE OF SHEWBREAD

Hebrews chapter 9 begins by saying that "even the first covenant had ordinances of divine service." The writer is emphasizing that if the Old Covenant had them, then certainly the New Covenant does. There were certain things to be done in the service of God, and these are what we are now considering in our study of the Tabernacle. What can we learn from this great parable about our service toward God?

We now come to the golden table of shewbread which stood on the right-hand side as the priest entered through the screen into the holy place. It was made of acacia wood covered with pure gold, and it tells us of Jesus, the Son of God, His High Priestly title, you remember, the Man in the glory. He is there supporting His people in their service Godward. It had a double crown, reminding us that the Lord Jesus is a Priest for ever after the order of Melchizedek, who was king of Salem and priest of God Most High. Normally those two offices were never combined in one person. King Uzziah attempted to do priestly work and he died of leprosy. That honour is reserved for the Lord Jesus and there is a precious verse in Zechariah chapter 6 which speaks of the Lord Jesus in a future day as a Priest upon His throne and it says the counsel of peace shall be between

98

them both. The Kingly crown and the Priestly crown both belong to Him, and our priesthood takes character from the One who is great Priest over God's house.

You will notice in 1 Peter 2 we are described in verse 5 as a holy priesthood and in verse 9 as a royal priesthood, because God has set our High Priest as King upon His holy hill of Zion. The golden table was for holding the shewbread, twelve loaves representing the twelve tribes. They were brought fresh each sabbath day and laid in two rows and then covered with frankincense. And God said, "they shall set upon the table bread before Me always" (Exodus 25:30). It is interesting because shewbread literally means bread of the faces and there is no doubt God saw Israel typified in those loaves.

King Balak tried to get Balaam to curse God's people but he could not do so; God put remarkable words of blessing into Balaam's mouth and on one of those occasions he said, "He has not beheld iniquity in Jacob, neither has He seen perverseness in Israel" (Numbers 23:21). But they were a perverse people as we know, and many times they grieved God's heart by their constant grumbling. Obviously when He put those words into Balaam's mouth He was viewing them in all the perfection of His Son, of which those twelve loaves of meal offering spoke to Him. It is true of us, too, for God sees us in Christ, holy and without blemish before Him in love. Hebrews chapter 9:24 says that Christ has entered "into heaven itself, now to appear before the face of God for us." Isn't that just exceedingly precious? Christ before God's face on our behalf and we are seen in Him in all His perfections.

The twelve loaves made of fine flour, which had been bruised and crushed and then submitted to the heat of the oven, was Israel's meal offering and they tell us about the Lord Jesus in His life before God. The scripture says He was made "perfect through sufferings" (Hebrews 2:10). Not that there was ever any imperfection in Him for He was altogether holy, but all the crushing and bruising experiences through which He passed only served to bring all His perfections into clearer view. God feasted on those perfections for seven days and then on the sabbath, when the fresh loaves were ready for the table, the priest took his golden spoon, scooped off the frankincense and burned it on the golden altar.

The scripture in Leviticus chapter 24 says it was "for a memorial, even an offering made by fire unto the LORD." 'Memorial' comes from a word meaning 'to remember' so it was a remembrance offering; and the loaves became the food of the priests. In some way God kept it fresh, I feel sure, and they were to eat it in a holy place, for it was part of their holy service. So we see them having communion with God in relation to the table, described as the pure table before the Lord. "My table," God calls it in Ezekiel chapter 44. We cannot fail to see the connection between this and the table of communion God has set in His house today.

It provides us also with a weekly service, for the disciples in the churches of God in New Testament days kept it each Lord's day. That is clear from Acts chapter 20; and in 1 Corinthians chapter 11 Paul refers to it as "the table of the Lord." Never is it referred to as the Father's table, as we sometimes hear. It is the Lord's table and those who acknowledge the Lordship of Christ by obedience to His Word are invited to it. It is priestly service and brings us back again to 1 Peter 2:5, "You also, as living stones, are built up a spiritual house, to be a holy priesthood, to offer up spiritual sacrifices, acceptable to God through Jesus Christ."

What a very precious time it is on Lord's day morning when we gather around the Lord's table to remember our Lord Jesus in the broken bread and the out-poured cup. "This do in remembrance of Me," He said. It is a time when we commune with God His Father, enjoying with Him the excellencies of His Son - almost as though we are taking our golden spoon and offering something of the sweetness of the frankincense to God, some precious thoughts of Christ we have gleaned during the previous week.

It is a time of sweetest communion. "The cup of blessing which we bless, is it not a communion of the blood of Christ? The bread which we break, is it not a communion of the body of Christ?" asks Paul in 1 Corinthians 10. There is no doubt that the time spent around the table of the Lord is the finest time of the week and if we are wise we shall make careful preparation for it, preparing not only our own hearts, so that we may be cleansed of defilement, but preparing also some precious thoughts of Christ which we can offer as spiritual sacrifices to His God and Father.

23

THE GOLDEN LAMPSTAND

We now come in our study of the Tabernacle to the lampstand which stood on the left-hand side as the priest entered the holy place. It was made of a talent of pure gold, beaten into its intricate shape by the goldsmith's hammer, and obviously men like Bezalel and Oholiab were specially gifted for their task. The result of their finished work was a beautiful lampstand, sometimes referred to as a candlestick: but that is a mistake, for it was a stand for holding lamps which burned with olive oil to give light in God's sanctuary. It had a centre shaft and three branches on each side and on top of each rested a golden lamp, seven in all. If the priests were to serve in God's house they needed light and this was God's way of providing light in His holy place.

We have seen clearly the other items of furniture in the holy place were made of acacia wood overlaid with pure gold and there is no difficulty in seeing in them a beautiful picture of our Lord Jesus in various aspects of His service in the presence of God. But this lampstand had no wood in it. It was pure gold, and I suggest to you it speaks to us of the Holy Spirit whom we know is the great witness-bearer. "He shall bear witness of Me," the Lord Jesus said. Remembering the Tabernacle was a copy and shadow of heavenly things, we ask was there something in heaven which corresponded to this? There was indeed! In Revelation chapter 4, John tells us that when a door was opened in heaven he saw seven lamps of fire burning before God's throne which are the seven spirits of God. We know there is only one Holy Spirit, of course, but the seven lamps speak of the perfection of His activities.

Then in Revelation chapter 1 John saw seven lampstands and in the midst of them one like the Son of Man clothed with a garment down to the feet. The Lord Jesus is seen walking in the midst of the golden lampstands and we are distinctly told ''The seven lampstands are seven churches.'' Then He proceeded to give John a message to be written to each of these churches of God. And that fits beautifully into the parable presented to us, for in those apostolic days how did the Holy Spirit send out the light of divine truth except through disciples gathered together in the churches of God? So it opens up a most precious line of truth as we contemplate the possibility of being a golden lamp shining with others on a lampstand and together sending out, by the Holy Spirit's enabling, the light of divine truth.

You will remember John the Baptist was described as a lamp that burned and shone. Warmth and light came from that holy life, but his was a unique ministry as forerunner of the Lord Jesus and in a sense he served alone. We are not called to serve alone today. The New Testament scriptures make it abundantly clear that God wants us to serve together, with other like-minded ones who acknowledge the authority of the Lord Jesus, and each as lamps burning and shining on the lampstand all of gold.

But, you say, the lamps were also made of gold, beaten out of the same talent of pure gold. True, they were and every child of God, born again by the work of God's Holy Spirit is a partaker of the divine nature, and that new creation in us is all of God all pure gold. We know only too well there's still the old nature present in us, so prone to sin, and that's why we often feel the tug-of-war, the flesh lusting against the Spirit and the Spirit against the flesh, as Galatians chapter 5 describes it. But it's the part of us which answers to the gold, the new nature through which the Holy Spirit works.

Zechariah chapter 4 presents a lovely picture of a lampstand all of gold with its seven lamps and a bowl on the top. There were two olive trees, one each side, representing the two leaders Zerubbabel and Joshua, who led the people when they were rebuilding God's house, when they returned from Babylon. It says that through these two olive branches the golden oil was poured which kept the light burning on the lampstand. And the message to them through the angel was: "Not by might, nor by power, but by My Spirit, saith the LORD of hosts." It is as true today as it was in that day, or at any time when God's servants are doing His work, it will only go forward in the power of the Holy Spirit. It is not by our own efforts but by His working through us that the light will shine.

And notice, please, in this great parable we are studying that the lampstand stood in the holy place and the priests served in its light at the golden altar which teaches us about the assembly prayers, and at the table of the Lord which held the shewbread and from which we learn precious lessons about the breaking of bread. It is all exceedingly precious and I leave it with You for your meditation. May the Lord the Spirit, the great witness Bearer guide you into all the truth as the Lord Jesus promised He would.

24

THE ARK AND THE MERCY SEAT

We now come in our study of the Tabernacle to the most sacred part of all, within the veil where only the high priest was allowed to enter, and then only one day in the year and not without blood, as Hebrews chapter 9 puts it. Verse 6 says "the priests go in continually into the first tabernacle, accomplishing the services; but into the second the high priest alone, once in the year, not without blood which he offers for himself, and for the errors of the people: the Holy Spirit thus signifying that the way into the holy place has not yet been made manifest, while as the first tabernacle is still standing." It is not standing now, of course; that is past and gone, for the Most High no longer dwells in a temple made with hands. That ended when Christ died and the visible sign for all to see was the rending of the veil from the top to the bottom.

But we learn valuable lessons from these Old Testament shadows which help us in regard to our service today in God's spiritual house, comprised of living stones, obedient disciples together in testimony. So let us take a look inside the most holy place. We find it contained the ark of the covenant made of acacia wood, telling of Christ's perfect humanity, and overlaid inside and outside with pure gold, so it speaks to us of Christ in glory, the One who in all things has been given the pre-eminence. And on top of the ark and serving as a cover, was a slab of pure gold called the mercy seat and the fact that no measurements are given as to its thickness may well remind us that the depth of God's mercy is beyond measure. Inside the ark were placed the two tables of stone on which the ten commandments were written. Inside that ark they were kept intact and it is a beautiful picture of Christ, for who but He was ever able to keep God's law perfectly? "I delight to do Your will, O God; yea, Your law is within My heart" were words David wrote about Him in Psalm 40.

At each end of the mercy seat and of one piece with it were golden cherubim with their wings spread out as though they were covering it. And indeed they were, for from other scriptures we learn they were the guardians of God's holiness. They surrounded the throne of God just as they did in this lovely parable of things in heaven. And God's presence was between those cherubim and upon the mercy seat was where God's presence was. "There I will meet with you, and I will commune with you from above the mercy seat, from between the two cherubim which are upon the ark of the testimony" (Exodus 25:22).

But how could a holy God dwell among a people who failed so often and proved themselves again and again so completely unable to keep the commandments contained inside the ark? That His presence was there, was indicated by the pillar of cloud by day and the pillar of fire by night. Israel knew the living God was dwelling in their midst, but I ask again, how was it possible, when God was so holy and they were so failing?

The answer lies in the fact that it was a blood-stained mercy seat. On the great day of atonement, that day which was so special in Israel's year, the high priest went into the very presence of God, inside the veil, creating first of all another veil as it were, for he went in burning sweet incense that he die not, the scripture says. So I do not think he ever clearly the throne of God. And he came in with blood of a bullock for his own personal sin offering, reminding us he also was a failing man; and then finally he entered with the blood of the goat, sin offering for the people, and each time he sprinkled the blood on the mercy seat and seven times in front of it. So God looked down on a blood-stained mercy seat, and by reason of the blood shed, pointing forward to the great sacrifice of His own dear Son, He was content to dwell amongst them for another year.

Oh, what precious truth it is; for Hebrews chapter 9 says "but through His own blood" Christ "entered in once for all into the holy place, having obtained eternal redemption." And He is there now on God's throne, our great High Priest, now to appear before the face of God for us. When Christ died at Calvary the veil of the temple was rent from the top to the bottom, showing that God had finished with the old order of things. His presence was no longer there. But Christ has entered into the holy place above, and He has gone in as a Forerunner because we are invited to enter too. That is the great teaching of Hebrews chapter 10. Verse 19 says "Having therefore, brethren, boldness to enter into the holy place by the blood of Jesus." Not now confined to one man once in the year, but all His priests together as a priesthood, for He has "made us a kingdom and priests unto His God and Father" (Revelation 1:6).

We have access into the holy place in heaven, to offer up spiritual sacrifices acceptable to God through Jesus Christ. Some, when referring to the breaking of bread service speak of Christ being in their midst, in fulfillment of the Matthew chapter 18 scripture, "where two or three are gathered together in My name, there am I in the midst of them." But if you read it carefully you will see that the context does not deal with our times of assembly worship. No, it is a loftier truth than that of Matthew

18. For when we gather to remember the Lord Jesus we enter in spirit into the very presence of God, "by the Way which He dedicated for us, a new and living Way, through the veil, that is to say, His flesh; and having a great Priest over the house of God, let us draw near with a true heart in fulness of faith" (Hebrews 10:20,21).

I am quite sure this has to do with the breaking of bread on the Lord's Day morning, the loaf reminding us there is an un-rent veil in heaven, the human body of Christ. If He was not there we could never draw near. And the cup of wine speaking of His blood and telling us so eloquently that into God's presence He has entered as a Forerunner in all the value of His blood shed at Calvary. Oh, what glorious truth it is - and we are only scratching the surface of it in our brief study, but hopefully whetting your appetite to look into it more carefully. I do believe it is precious truth God wants us to put into practice as we worship Him, and I ask that you prayerfully consider it as you study these portions in the epistle to the Hebrews.

The hymn writer has captured the thought in the hymn we sometimes sing at our breaking of bread service:

The holies now we enter,

In perfect peace with God,

Regaining the lost centre,

Through Christ's atoning blood.

Though great may be our dullness

In thought and word and deed,

We glory in the fulness

Of Him Who meets our need.

Much incense is ascending

Before the eternal throne
God graciously is bending
To listen to his own
Though feeble are our praises
Christ adds his sweet perfume
And love the censer raises
Their odours to consume.

O God, we come with singing
Because our great High Priest
Our names to Thee is bringing
And ne'er forgets the least.
For us He wears the mitre,
Where holiness shines bright,
For us, His robes are whiter
Than heaven's unsullied light.
(J. Dorricott)

ABOUT THE PUBLISHER

Hayes Press (www.hayespress.org) is a registered charity in the United Kingdom, whose primary mission is to disseminate the Word of God, mainly through literature. It is one of the largest distributors of gospel tracts and leaflets in the United Kingdom, with over 100 titles and many thousands dispatched annually. In addition to paperbacks and eBooks, Hayes Press also publishes Plus Eagles' Wings, a fun and educational Bible magazine for children, and Golden Bells, a popular daily Bible reading calendar in wall or desk formats.

If you would like to contact Hayes Press, there are a number of ways you can do so:

By mail: c/o The Barn, Flaxlands, Royal Wootton Bassett, Wiltshire, UK SN4 8DY

By phone: 01793 850598

By eMail:info@hayespress.org

via Facebook: www.facebook.com/hayespress.org

MORE TITLES FROM ALAN TOMS

LESSONS FROM ELIJAH AND ELISHA

Elijah and Elisha are two of the most significant people in the Old Testament. Alan recounts the major events from their lives and brings out some important lessons today for any Christian who wants to serve God like they did - lessons about faith, trust, obedience, knowing God's will in the ups and downs of life.

WHERE IS GOD'S HOUSE TODAY?

Is God is dwelling among men on earth today? Where is His dwelling place? How may I be sure of a place in it? This book was written because believers want to know the answers to these important questions. It looks firstly at the Old Testament - remembering that 'whatsoever things were written before were written for our learning' (Romans 15:4) and that the tabernacle which Moses built is said in the New Testament to be a symbol or parable for the present time (Hebrews 9:9). As these lessons are applied to what is written in the New Testament, the author's prayer is that God's Holy Spirit will make clear the lessons He wants believers to learn in regard to the worship and service of God today.